THANKS

IIIIIIIIIIIIIII FOR THE IIIIIIIIIIIIIII

MONEY

G. P. PUTNAM'S SONS ⑤ NEW YORK

THANKS
|||||||||||||| FOR THE ||||||||||||||
MONEY

HOW TO USE MY LIFE STORY
TO BECOME THE BEST
JOEL McHALE
✳ YOU CAN BE ✳

DICTATED, BUT NOT READ, BY **JOEL McHALE**

WITH A FOREWORD BY **JOEL McHALE**

COMPILED AND HEAVILY REVISED BY BRAD STEVENS AND BOYD VICO
BUT MOSTLY BY **JOEL McHALE**

G. P. PUTNAM'S SONS
Publishers Since 1838
An imprint of Penguin Random House LLC
375 Hudson Street
New York, New York 10014

Library of Congress Cataloging-in-Publication Data
Names: McHale, Joel, author. | Stevens, Brad, compiler. | Vico,
Boyd, compiler.
Title: Thanks for the money : how to use my life story to become the best
Joel McHale you can be / dictated, but not read, by Joel McHale ; with a
foreword by Joel McHale ; compiled and heavily revised by Brad Stevens and
Boyd Vico but mostly by Joel McHale.
Description: New York : G. P. Putnam's Sons, 2016.
Identifiers: LCCN 2016027548 | ISBN 9780399575372
Subjects: LCSH: McHale, Joel. | Comedians—United States—Biography. |
Actors—United States—Biography.
Classification: LCC PN2287.M5458 A3 2016 | DDC 791.4302/8092 [B] —dc23
LC record available at https://lccn.loc.gov/2016027548
p.   cm.

Printed in the United States of America
1   3   5   7   9   10   8   6   4   2

BOOK DESIGN BY MEIGHAN CAVANAUGH

CONTENTS

Twenty-Three Chapters That, When Assembled, Meet a Publisher's Minimum Requirement for a Celebrity Memoir/Self-Help Book

|||||||| **PART I** ||||||||

WE'LL GET TO YOU IN A MINUTE, BUT FIRST——*ME*

THANKS

IIIIIIIIIIIII FOR THE IIIIIIIIIIIII

MONEY

FOREWORD

You never forget that moment when your life changes forever. It leaves a lasting mark—like the deep groove carved into sequoia bark by a logger's hatchet, the shimmering black sands that whisper of a millennia-old volcanic eruption, or the crescent-shaped scars from your multiple calf implant surgeries.

Everything seemed so perfect on that sun-dappled, breeze-kissed, nice-smelling afternoon. As I am wont to do in my downtime, I was drinking and staring into the middle distance. I had devoted most of the morning to dwelling on professional disagreements and some mild career envy, and as a result, I was tired. That lady I married was reading a book in the shade as our two young sons played in the pool of our new home.

Being surrounded by those I love had brought me a sense of . . . I don't want to say "satisfaction," because that makes me think of two things: the emotional state of satisfaction, which I define as a cowardly capitulation to inner peace, and also *Satisfaction*, the criminally overlooked 1988 musical drama starring Justine Bateman and Liam Neeson. I loved that film, but it never caught on at the box office—at least, not domestically. I understand that it's the highest-grossing film of all time in Estonia.

I had finally come to terms with the state of Justine Bateman's film career and taken a celebratory swig of single-malt Scotch when my eldest son, Boy 1, innocently called out, "Daddy, I can touch the bottom."

"That's great, First Boy," I murmured into my drink. "You sure have grown up fast." That's the kind of rapport I share with my children. We have great talks.

"No, Daddy—everywhere. Everywhere I walk in our pool, I can touch the bottom."

A sudden panic washed over me, like a wave of hot turkey gravy. My throat tightened. My left arm went numb. I could smell nothing but the unmistakable odor of burnt hair. "You were having a stroke, Joel," is what you might be saying. In which case, I would reply, "Gee, I didn't know you were a doctor. Let me finish my story."

"Look at me! My feet are flat on the bottom of the pool, and my head is above the water!" My son's infectious joy sickened me. He paraded back and forth, waving his hands, making a real show of it. "Yay! Look at me!" Each step was a tiny foot-dagger in my heart.

I lurched out of my chair and staggered across the grounds of my home, which is a collection of fancy words for "lawn," over to the car park, which is what we call our driveway, and made sick all over the hood of my Porsche, which is actually the trunk.

That lady I married appeared at my elbow with great concern. "What is it, Joel? Why did you vomit?" That's the kind of rapport I share with that lady I married. We have great talks.

"That kid in the pool is right," I barked, dabbing at my chin. "We have no deep end. It's all one . . . one . . ."

She placed a warm palm against the small of my back. "Joel, take a breath. Find your words."

"It's all one depth!" I shrieked, and the tears came, hot and fast, dribbling down my face like salty rivulets of turkey gravy.

How did I let this happen?

How could I even *think* of purchasing a new home with an in-ground pool that possessed no deep end? How could I even *entertain* the thought of a pool that doesn't allow for reverse dives, inward dives, jackknifes, or even that lowest form of water sports japery, the cannonball?

After years of hard work, and perseverance, and screaming at people on various phone calls, I had done the unthinkable and *settled*. As a professional actor, stand-up comedian, and basic-cable television host, I had never settled for anything less than the best. Other than that time I agreed to become a basic-cable television host.

"Is everything all right?" a soft voice queried. It was Mateo, my loyal manservant. We have a running joke where he repeatedly asks that I not refer to him as a "manservant," or "Mateo." But this was no time for our classic "I'm a landscaper, and my name is Hector" routine.

I grabbed Mateo roughly by his lapels. Yes, I make my support staff dress in formal attire. I don't know why everyone makes a big deal out of it. Anyway, I grabbed Mateo roughly by his lapels—so roughly, in fact, that his cummerbund came loose. "Cut off my balls, Mateo," I hissed at him.

"Mr. Joel—please, not this again." He was trembling.

"Take those hedge clippers and chop off my penis and my testicles. You'll do it if you love me." At this point, that lady I married had spirited Boy 1 and Other Boy back into the house. I could hear the hydraulic hiss of the panic room door sealing shut, even over Mateo's blubbery protestations.

"Mr. Joel, Mr. Joel—please. The pool can be fixed. It can be done. You just need to *dig a deeper pool.*"

I released him. He was right. The problem—like others detailed in the pages ahead—was challenging but ultimately surmountable. And the solution—like many more detailed in the pages ahead—was to rent a backhoe.

I let out a long sigh of relief and, with great effort, tucked my genitals back into my pants. I cupped Mateo's sweet, beefy, sunburned face in my hands, gave him a soft peck on the cheek, and straightened his top hat.

I would do it. I would dig a deeper pool. This endeavor would require money, of course, and a grueling, nearly five-minute Internet search to determine a baseline construction price, and . . . holy *fuck*—it is really costly. Believe me, I shopped around. I got at least three different estimates. Those short-term backhoe renters are *bloodsuckers.*

"It's too expensive . . . it's too expensive . . . it's too expensive . . . it's too expensive . . ." It was the voice of that lady I married, echoing in my head. She was saying something about this newer, deeper pool being a "fool's errand" and an "unwise expenditure" and how there wasn't enough "potable water in the panic room."

She was right on all counts, as I would learn much later. But in the short term, I needed a new revenue stream. Sure, I had conquered television—both real and cable. I had mildly defeated the world of cinema—both theatrical and straight-to-video. And I had bent the world of comedy over my knee and made it call me "the Harbormaster." But this pool thing would require a new, uncharted course.

I was good at talking, that much was certain. But how could I turn the words I usually talked into a permanent thing that people could purchase at a wildly inflated price?

And then it dawned on me. A pile of pages with words on them, bound together to give some semblance of coherence.

That's right: *a book.*

But what sells? Tell-all memoirs, mawkish self-help guides, and stories about teenagers in postapocalyptic death tournaments. It was settled—I would write a book that would feature all of those things.

I would reveal heretofore private tales of my youth: how and when I got my infamous eyebrow scar, where and why I lost my virginity, and whether or not these both happened during the same Bible camp canoe trip.

As with any semirespectable tell-all, I would include an unflinching chronicle of my weeks-long struggle to earn a living as a professional actor. And I would spin great tales of Hollywood excess—the parties, the after-parties, the orgies, the after-orgies, and the private, celebrity-only footwear-release events/orgies.

Then, for the betterment of all, I would impart the wisdom of my experiences. The attentive reader would learn from my triumphs, take heed of my missteps, and maintain a running tally of the book's frequent grammatical errors.

It would be everything one could possibly want in a book (including bonus charts and illustrations!), because Joel McHale doesn't do things half-assed. Joel McHale uses the whole ass, just like the Native Americans used to when they wrote *their* showbiz memoirs.

My book would help me dig a bigger, better, and deeper pool. And as a side bonus, it would also help dig a bigger, better, and deeper you.

I sat down and opened my laptop, which I had slammed shut after the initial shock of the pool renovation costs. But now my frustration was gone, and in its place—inspiration. The words tumbled out of me, hot and fast and chunky, like so much turkey gravy.

The book . . . *had already begun.*

—Joel McHale
Goldeneye Estate, Jamaica
August 13, 1964

PART I

WE'LL GET TO YOU IN A MINUTE, BUT FIRST—*ME*

THE LIFE AND ADVENTURES OF JOEL McHALE

THE BEAST AWAKENS

CHILDHOOD STORIES THAT GIVE THE
IMPRESSION THAT I AM RELATABLE AND DECENT

'll always remember the exact moment when I was born into a life of artistic expression. I was naked, curled up in a ball, in a cramped, dark room. I could hear the muffled sounds of a crowd murmuring expectantly. Then someone grabbed me by my neck and skull and yanked me into the light. I was covered in blood and surrounded by large, looming figures in surgical scrubs. I heard tears, laughter, and my father exclaiming, "Honey, look at his little penis."

The year was 1995, and it was the opening-night performance of *I, Zygote*, an experimental musical about the rigors of childbirth. I was playing the pivotal role of Fetus #2. Noted theater critic Ray Stodell called the production "a competently staged yet showy, overwrought mess. Two stars."

But in many ways, my career as a performer actually started twenty-four years earlier, under completely different circumstances. I was naked, curled up in a ball, and pulled into the light of a hospital room. There were tears and laughter. Someone said something about my penis. I had been born—literally this time.

Yet again, I was playing the pivotal role of Fetus #2 (we had to share the room due to hospital overcrowding issues). Noted theater critic Ray Stodell referred to my birth as "a competently staged yet showy, overwrought mess. Two stars." Ray is a family friend with very little awareness of personal boundaries.

The bright lights, the constant attention, the people checking me for basic reflexes and motor skills—this was truly my first taste of celebrity. And I was hooked! . . . up to a machine that monitored my vital signs.

A few days later, a kindly man and woman took me home. Once my brain grew enough to retain memories, I came to know these people as Laurie and Jack McHale, my parents. I was born to these wonderful, pale, strong-jawlined people in Rome, Italy. Yes, the same city that created the world's most widely utilized alphabet, instituted the concept of the three-course meal, and produced some of the most amazing architecture in human history is also the birthplace of the *Soup* guy.

My Italian toddlerhood was a magical, picturesque experience. I developed the ability to grasp and hold things while cradling a *doppio* espresso in the Piazza della Rotonda. My basic language and comprehension skills were honed by correcting tourists who dared to mispronounce "gnocchi."[1] And I learned the concept of object permanence while decoding ciphers alongside a noted Harvard

---

[1] The "g," the second "c," and the "i" are all silent.

symbologist during his efforts to expose a vast cover-up within the Vatican.

I wish I could tell you I was born in Rome because my dad was an art thief or because my mom was an international assassin. Like you, I secretly wish my parents were criminals.[2] Cool criminals, like Casey Affleck in *Ocean's Eleven*, and not petty crooks, like Scott Caan in *Ocean's Twelve*. But no, my parents had dumb, dependable jobs—the kind that eventually pull you away from all the obnoxious, in-your-face beauty, history, and culture of Rome.

My dad worked as the dean of students for the Loyola University Rome Center,[3] and my mom was a Canadian student matriculating abroad in Italy when they met. Whoa, whoa, whoa—lower that arched eyebrow. There was nothing weird about it. They were much closer in age than you think: my mom was twelve, and my dad was fourteen. Yeah, he was a real prodigy in the dean-of-students game. Okay, I'm lying. They were both in their twenties, living the high life in Rome in the 1960s. This was the *La Dolce Vita* era, which is an Italian phrase that means "unlimited breadsticks."

So those are the loins that produced me: those of a college administrator and a Canadian student. Oh, and my mom's dad—my grandfather—helped monitor fish populations for the United

---

[2] If your parents actually *are* criminals, you should know that I firmly believe in the old adage "The apple doesn't fall far from the tree." Which reminds me—DID YOU ACTUALLY PAY FOR THIS BOOK?! Oh yeah? Well, what about that apple you're holding!? I'm supposed to believe that it just "fell from that tree"?!

[3] Home of the Chargin' Caligulas.

Nations.[4] Obviously, I was destined for a career in the entertainment industry.

I was the middle child, between two brothers—additional sons whom, I assume, my parents had in order to provide me with easily harvestable replacement organs. We were just a young, pale, carefree family enjoying a comfortable life in Rome.[5] I mean, it was comfortable for *me*, because I didn't have to worry about paying bills. But my dad made very little money, my mom's side career of being ogled by Italian men smoking in outdoor cafés wasn't a reliable source of income, and my one-year-old brother, Stephen, just laid around, acting like his dumb baby neck couldn't support the weight of his skull—you know, like a real good-for-nothing deadbeat.

Yes, the career of a dean of students for the European annex of an American college is an unpredictable, rough-and-tumble one—so my family headed stateside when I was three. The move to America ensured that my brothers and I could be closer to our extended family while at the same time never experiencing the carnal pleasures of uninhibited Italian women. I still hold this against my father, my mother, and, for some reason, my youngest brother and his dumb baby neck.

There's really no telling where I'd be now if my family had stayed put in Italy. Maybe I'd have hosted the long-running pop culture clip show *The Minestrone* or played the rakish lawyer Gio Vingario on the beloved but low-rated Italian sitcom *Comunità*. Or perhaps I'd be a semiretired art historian, like Julia Roberts in *Ocean's Twelve*.

---

[4] Sorry to get all "name-droppy" so early in the book. Matt Damon told me not to do that.
[5] Which explains Rome's official motto: "When you're here, you're family."

But really, the only benefit of my birth in Rome—other than the precious gift of life—was a solid opening line for my Wikipedia entry. Which, in turn, gives any lazy journalist a softball question for interviews, if they've decided "Did you *really* bite Chevy Chase?" is too confrontational.[6]

So thank you, Rome—for giving me the opportunity to constantly name-drop my birthplace. And thank you, dear reader, for asking me to bring it up. That was really nice of you. *Arrivederci!*[7]

---

[6] For more information on this subject, please consult chapter 17 and its section entitled "How to Survive a Chevy Chase Attack."

[7] Or in English, "The bottomless salad is complimentary with your entrée."

2

SOME STUFF ABOUT MY PARENTS

A PASSIVE-AGGRESSIVE GLIMPSE AT THE PEOPLE
I WILL EVENTUALLY TURN INTO

owe a lot to my parents: a happy childhood, a strong sense of self, the pride of fiscal responsibility, that twenty bucks they loaned me for headshots when I was a struggling actor,[1] two brothers whom I occasionally love dearly, and what many medical professionals have pointed out is an "alarmingly strong" genetic tolerance for mixing alcohol types. My parents are truly great people.

Now let's talk about *your* parents. Yes, we have to. I want you to imagine your parents having sex. Yes, you have to. In fact, the very act of trying *not* to envision your mom and dad, in the prime of their lives, humping like jackrabbits will lead to you picturing that very thing. Probably because I keep describing it.

Your parents.

Having sex.

You just imagined it again, didn't you?

---

[1] I swear I will pay you back. I'm currently on a fixed income.

The reason I bring the aforementioned imagery of *your* parents[2] having sweaty, angry sex on the kitchen floor of the home you were raised in is because it's something that I often think about. No, not *your* parents banging, you sicko! *My* parents—Laurie and Jack McHale.

I have a theory that the way in which our parents have sex can dictate[3] our future course—that the very position in which their young, supple, sweaty bodies were entwined when they reached mutual orgasm guides every facet of their offspring's lives. Why are you suppressing your gag reflex right now? Your parents are sexual creatures, and I think it's time—here in the opening pages of a book I expect you to read to completion—you reckon with that.

I want you to do something else for me, other than yet again imagining your mother and father engaged in hot sexual congress while you're at soccer practice.[4] Next time you're at a family gathering, ask your parents for some explicit details about the night you were conceived. Make sure other people (ideally siblings or family friends) are within earshot to serve as supplemental witnesses. What you'll learn—about your parents, their bedroom proclivities, and the destiny forged by both—will amaze and confound you.[5]

Maybe what would make this easier and more palatable—and also help prove my theory—are some detailed illustrations of my own parents in various sexual positions.

---

[2] Deb and Mike.

[3] Or "dick-tate," tee-hee!

[4] Remember? You came home and your mom was sweaty, and when you asked her about it, she just said she'd been "moving some stuff around in the garage."

[5] And possibly ruin Thanksgiving dinner, but that's not on me.

JOEL McHALE'S MAMA-AND-PAPA SUTRA!

Here are my parents in the classic missionary position. Honest, forthright, with an unshakable faith in the simple, unadorned act of fornication. The result? My younger brother, Stephen, who grew up to become a priest. That's right: A *LITERAL* MISSIONARY.

Ah, yes. The spirited "jackhammer" position, which was attempted after my dad had four gin rickeys at an office Christmas party. Certainly this act of lovemaking would produce a child who is handy and accomplished with plug insertion. That's right: my older brother, Christopher, who is A LICENSED ELECTRICIAN.

And here are my beloved parents, Laurie and Jack McHale, on Valentine's night 1971—performing what many refer to as "the Reverse Cowgirl." This is probably the most flamboyant and attention-getting sexual position of all. And the result? That's right: me, Joel McHale—ACTOR, COMEDIAN, ENTERTAINER, and FEARLESS INVESTIGATOR OF PARENTAL SEX HABITS.[6]

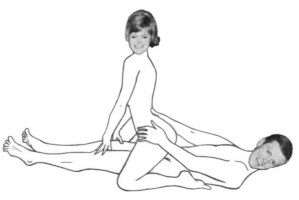

---

[6] And now, PUBLISHED AUTHOR.

I think you'll agree that my theory has been proven, and as a result, I have burned through one page of my contractually required book length. From here on out, I will no longer ask you to envision your own parents grunting and shuddering as they bring each other to heights of sexual ecstasy on the family couch. Yes—the same couch you all sit on when you open Christmas presents together.[7]

My parents are amazing, hilarious, and tolerant. For proof, I submit the previous page, where they legally permitted me to print images of them having sex. But what are these incredible people like when they are fully clothed? And no, I'm not talking about dry humping. That's a completely different theory, and frankly one that is not appropriate for a celebrity memoir.

My dad is insanely cheap. I wouldn't call him "frugal" or "thrifty"—that would suggest there's an awareness or motive behind his actions. No, he's so cheap that his behavior transcends simple fiscal moderation and suggests a worldview where currency itself has no meaning. The act of refusing to pay full price for goods and services is, in itself, the only thing of value to my father. Yeah. He's psychotically cheap. My dad is the Jeffrey Dahmer of cheapness—except he would never pay for an extra freezer to store human heads. (I love you, Dad. Just think of all the free dinners you're gonna get from the money I make on this book.)

When I was a kid, we had a cat named Ashley. For years, I assumed the cat was named for *Kiss the Girls* star Ashley Judd, but

---

[7] Sorry, my book contract also required a minimum of four increasingly detailed sex fantasies about the reader's own parents. The good people of G. P. Putnam's Sons are a bunch of pervs.

a quick IMDb search now suggests those dates couldn't possibly sync up.

We all loved Ashley the Cat.[8] She was a member of the family. She liked to play with my brother Stephen, and she'd often leave gifts of dead vermin on the back porch, just like my brother Chris did. But there was an issue. Ashley had terrible breath.

This was breath that went beyond normal pet breath, which we all know is inherently awful. It's not like you ever hear someone bragging about the quality of their pet's breath: "My boxer-pit mix, Duke, has the most sublime breath. Duke, come here and let the nice lady take a big whiff of your open mouth . . . See? Fresh sage, with notes of peppermint and dark stone fruits."

So you know Ashley's breath was bad because my dad actually agreed to take her to the vet to determine the cause. My brothers and I accompanied my dad and Ashley to the appointment. We got out of the car, and after Dad informed the cat that the mileage we'd just incurred would be docked from her daily ration of food, we went inside and had the following exchange:

MY DAD: Good afternoon, Doctor. Could you please perform a cost-efficient examination of this cat's teeth and gums?

JIFFY LUBE EMPLOYEE: Sir, this is a Jiffy Lube. The vet's office is two doors down.

MY DAD: Two doors down? I thought that was the locksmith.

JIFFY LUBE EMPLOYEE: No, that's in the other direction.

MY DAD: Hey, you're right. I guess I'm accustomed to getting my

---

[8] And yet we've always been split when it comes to the Judd.

sense of direction from looking *into* your establishment, whereas *your* point of view is informed by always looking out, toward the street—

JIFFY LUBE EMPLOYEE: Sir, I don't mean to be rude in front of you and your delightful little boy and these two street urchins, but could you please point that goddamned cat away from me? Its breath is fucking awful.

[*Five minutes later, at the actual veterinarian's office*]

MY DAD: Dr. Mandelcorn, thanks for seeing us. It's about—

VETERINARIAN: Your cat's breath, I know. It's fucking awful. I noticed the exam room door's paint bubbling and cracking from the outside. [*Performs cursory feline tooth and gum exam.*] By the way, your son is an incredibly magnetic personality. Funny, self-assured, with the charisma of a young Brando. And it's kind of you to give shelter to these other two. Anyway. Ashley the Cat's teeth are very dirty and will need to be cleaned.

MY DAD: [*long pause*] And what will that cost?

VETERINARIAN: Thirty dollars.

MY DAD: [*no pause*] And how much to put her to sleep?

VETERINARIAN: Fifteen.

Ashley the Cat survived that trip to the vet, but I'm not exaggerating when I tell you it was a disturbingly close call. In fact, the whole experience gave my dad some troubling new ideas about how to cut corners. In the days after that veterinarian appointment, I overheard him on a phone call, revising his will to stipulate that, in the event that he loses control over his faculties, he must be dressed in a man-sized cat suit and taken to Dr. Mandelcorn's for a simple fifteen-dollar procedure to end his suffering.

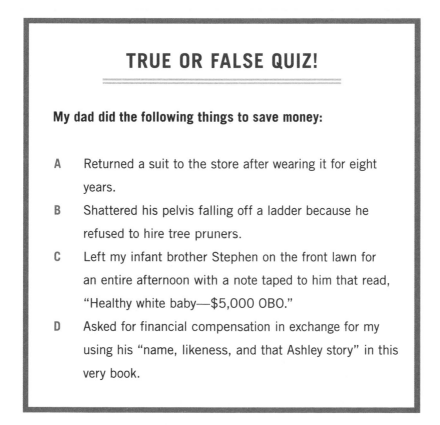

TRUE OR FALSE QUIZ!

My dad did the following things to save money:

A   Returned a suit to the store after wearing it for eight years.

B   Shattered his pelvis falling off a ladder because he refused to hire tree pruners.

C   Left my infant brother Stephen on the front lawn for an entire afternoon with a note taped to him that read, "Healthy white baby—$5,000 OBO."

D   Asked for financial compensation in exchange for my using his "name, likeness, and that Ashley story" in this very book.

A TRUE! B TRUE! C TRUE! D We haven't had this conversation yet, but I know it's coming, so . . . TRUE!

My mother is a perfect match for my dad.[9] Laurie McHale is, like her husband, lovely, pale, and accident-prone. She is also an incredibly supportive spouse. I witnessed this firsthand as a kid. In a typical relationship, there's a balance. One person is a hot-headed firebrand, while the other is calm and collected. One is obsessively tidy, while the other is a bit of a slob. And one is a suicidal Vietnam vet, while the other is a by-the-book family man with only two weeks until retirement. My point is that relationships usually have that balance, in order to forge a stronger bond, and to more effectively bring South African drug dealers to justice.

But not my parents. If someone cut my dad off while he was driving, my mom didn't offer a gentle pat on the shoulder and tell him not to lose his temper—she demanded that he follow the other driver home to "put the scare in him." You may think I'm exaggerating. After one incident of road rage, I actually heard my mom mutter to my father, *"Get 'em, Jack."*

But there's so much more to my mom than just childhood memories of her encouraging my father's violent retribution upon others. She is actually—driving habits excepted—the kindest, most decent person I have ever known. Like so many mothers, she held the family together. Laurie McHale was tasked with keeping four clumsy males—my father, me, and my brothers—from getting killed. I can't even keep track of the number of times she said things like, "Hey, maybe unplug that table saw before you climb on the

---

[9] Right down to blood type and liver compatibility. Believe me—he checked.

roof, Jack," or "I don't like the looks of that slow cooker, resting uneasily on the lip of that full tub you're about to step into, Chris," or "Boys, take off those capes before you play near the wood chipper okay?"

But my mom is not only nondumb—she is quietly brilliant. The kind of brilliance that sneaks up on you, after many decades of being preoccupied with boyhood things like roof climbs and playing on industrial farming equipment. She met my dad, in Rome, as a sweet, reserved Canadian girl. And like all Canucks, she was inherently intelligent and gullible. The intelligence stayed intact, but my dad's all-American playful dishonesty[10] eventually chipped away at her gullibility.

When you meet my parents,[11] you'll see what I mean. You can't get a straight, nonsarcastic answer out of my dad. When they were much younger, my parents were in Chicago, where my dad grew up. He gestured out at Lake Michigan and told my mom, "Hard to believe this was the site of one of the biggest naval battles of World War II, huh, Laurie?"

My mom blinked out at the lake. "Really, Jack?"

"Oh, sure—the Germans air-dropped hundreds of miniature submarines right here, into Lake Michigan." Being young and Canadian, my mother believed him. My dad laughed, and once she realized she had been fooled, my mother—again, being young and Canadian—apologized profusely.

---

[10] USA! USA! USA!

[11] They're swinging by later. So maybe clean yourself up a little.

My mom got used to these kinds of harmless flourishes and eventually came to appreciate them as part of my dad's very strange personality. She would later become a newspaper editor, back when there were still newspapers, and I can't help but think that her single-minded focus on factual accuracy is somehow informed by spending many years around my dad.

So my parents have always been this unstoppable force—a two-headed beast of love and support that is always out there, scanning the horizon for a deal on radial tires or one of those industrial tubs of mayonnaise they sell at Costco. If you ever encounter them, please remember: Use your turn signal. Otherwise, they will follow you home.

A HANDY CHECKLIST OF THINGS I INHERITED FROM MY PARENTS

- ☑ above-average height, below-average width
- ☑ love of the written word or some shit
- ☑ thick, flowing, lustrous head of hair[12]
- ☑ pretty good nipples
- ☑ hopefully some of their real estate holdings
- ☑ stupid, useless gallbladder
- ☑ pick up dry cleaning
- ☑ prehensile tail[13]
- ☑ love of checklists

---

[12] Fuck you. I know what you're thinking, and I talk about it later in the book.
[13] Sorry, Mom—but you knew this was a tell-all.

3

CHARMINGLY CALLOUS STORIES
OF A RECKLESS YOUTH

A CHAPTER DEDICATED TO THE MEMORY
OF MY THIRD BROTHER, DANNY

S o I've told you all about my parents, including the secret ritual they performed to ensure three masculine heirs to the McHale bloodline.[1] My brothers, Stephen and Christopher, were also born in Italy, but Stephen—being the youngest— was the only one who could never shake the accent.

When I was three, my parents packed up (Stephen was still small enough to fit inside a carry-on) and we moved to Seattle, Washington.[2] You could say this was motivated by my dad's career change and that, as a new executive for Weyerhaeuser,[3] he and his family needed to relocate near the company's headquarters in the Pacific Northwest. But my parents also knew that, with three young boys—

---

[1] Go back and look on page 17. It's there.
[2] I just want to point out, this was *way* before Seattle was considered cool. This was back when Macklemore was still a hair metal band.
[3] He still has to consult old business cards just to get the spelling correct.

all of us rambunctious and, as brothers, genetically driven to try to murder one another—the family might require the care and attention of American doctors to set our bones and stitch our limbs back together.

Young boys are like chimps: constantly shrieking, falling from trees, picking and eating insects from each other's fur, and—at the first sign of weakness—attacking with the goal of biting off fingers, faces, and genitals. My wife and I have two young sons of our own, and we always keep tranquilizer darts at the ready.

My older brother, Christopher, is a thoroughly decent human being. I know—weird, right? Chris is the hardest-working person I've ever been related to. He is also, hands down, the world's loudest conversationalist. As far as I know, he has excellent hearing. So I have no explanation for why, when you're talking to him—just the two of you, in a very quiet library or church pew—he feels the need to speak at a volume that is just below an actual shout. This can be tricky in everyday situations.

[*Me and Chris in a diner booth, circa 1988*]

ME: Chris, there's that cute girl from my pre-algebra class.

CHRIS: YOU SHOULD GO TALK TO HER, JOEL.

ME: [*whispering*] Chris—keep it down. Now she's looking over here.

CHRIS: YES, SHE'S LOOKING RIGHT AT YOU. I DON'T KNOW, JOEL. SHE HAS A PRETTY FACE BUT VERY, VERY [*somehow gets even louder*] LARGE THIGHS.

ME: [*slowly melts onto floor*]

CONSTRUCTION WORKER: [*barging in from outside*] Excuse me, could you guys keep it down? We're trying to jackhammer concrete out here.

I love my brother Chris. He's just a little loud sometimes.[4]

My younger brother, Stephen, is very different from Chris—in terms of both profession and general voice volume. As previously mentioned in that part of the book where I forced you (and my family) to imagine my parents having sex, Stephen is a fully licensed and bonded Episcopalian priest. How did the younger brother of a contractor/electrician and an actor/sex symbol become a man of the cloth? I can only assume that we, as Stephen's older brothers, laid claim to all the traits that were purely physical and greed-centric, so he was left with no other option than to make his life a beacon of faith and goodness. What a sucker.

For me, growing up with two brothers was great. And it was also like constantly cheating death. We'd play fun games, like Shoot a Hunting Arrow into the Air and Hope It Doesn't Hit One of Us, or Knife Catch (and its party game variation, Double Knife Catch), or How Much Blood Is in Stephen? But it rains a lot in Seattle, so sometimes we had to bust out the ol' board games. Many a soggy afternoon was spent inside playing Shoots and Ladders (you know, that game where you take turns firing a BB gun at whichever brother is attempting to climb a ladder).

I don't want you to think my parents were careless or inattentive.

---

[4] *Shhh.* Listen right now, and you'll hear him say, "IT'S TRUE, I AM" from somewhere in the Seattle suburbs.

In fact, they paid a lot of attention to us, usually organizing the neighborhood betting pool around which son would be next to be rushed to the emergency room. You have to understand—this was the late seventies and early eighties. It was the era of lawn darts and everyone smoking everywhere all the time. The only things that weren't covered in lead paint were children's seat belts—because they didn't exist.

When I was a toddler, a kid's seat belt was one of your parents casually reaching out to catch you as they slammed on the brakes.[5]

Here now is but a partial list of the head injuries that I, Joel McHale, endured while growing up.

Keep in mind, this is even before I played college football.[6]

THE MANY HEAD INJURIES OF YOUNG JOEL McHALE

#1 "The Skull Thickener"

TIME PERIOD: Preschool

INCIDENT REPORT: I was walking across this strange indoor ladder thing—which I assume was intended to test the average preschooler's ability to scale dangerous structures and absorb head injuries. I fell, on my head, and injured it.

---

[5] *"Get 'em, Jack."*

[6] Don't skip ahead, or you'll miss the gun story. Shit! Spoiler alert.

AVOIDABLE?: No, it was a strange indoor ladder thing and I was four.

AFTERMATH: Drowsiness, occasional loss of consciousness. Later: vomiting.

CONCUSSED?: Unknown (not taken to doctor)

#2: "Catch Me If You Can! (Seriously, I Am Falling from a Great Height)"

TIME PERIOD: Also preschool

INCIDENT REPORT: I fell from a cable rope swing and landed in a puddle, which did not cushion the impact of my head against the pavement, which was underneath said puddle.

AVOIDABLE?: You have to assume, right?

AFTERMATH: Wetness (from puddle, and head blood)

CONCUSSED?: Findings inconclusive (not taken to doctor)

#3: "Bunk-Deathbed"

TIME PERIOD: Young adolescence

INCIDENT REPORT: Fell out of new bunk bed, purchased days before by my father at a garage sale. The bunk bed was obtained at an irresistible discount because it was missing a guardrail for the top bunk. Also, I hit a chair on the way down. With my skull.

AVOIDABLE?: Yes. My brother Chris had fallen out of the same top bunk the night before, also sustaining a head injury. Neighbors a block away heard Chris whisper, "I THINK I AM FALLING OUT OF THE BED" seconds before his impact.

AFTERMATH: I was discovered on the floor of the bathroom, in a (small) pool of my own blood.

CONCUSSED?: Never found out (not taken to doctor). (OH, COME ON—THIS IS GETTING RIDICULOUS.)

#4 through #9: "The Great Fog"

TIME PERIOD: Mid-adolescence

INCIDENT REPORT: I don't have any recollection of these individual head injuries. But I was told they occurred by friends, emergency medical technicians, and the producers of Fox's *Most Insane Teenager Head Traumas* special in 2006.

AVOIDABLE?: Probably not. I now believe that the Angel of Death has been trying to collect my soul for years, through a series of increasingly elaborate "accidents," just like in the *Final Destination* films.

AFTERMATH: Career in entertainment industry

CONCUSSED?: For fuck's sake, yes. Numerous times.

#10: "Black Diamond"

TIME PERIOD: Fourteen years old

INCIDENT REPORT: I collided with another skier while hurtling down a slope. This was the "pre-helmet" era of winter sports, so it is likely we both collided while trying to avoid the prone, mangled figures of other unconscious skiers. We both sprung back up, assured each other that we were fine, and went our separate ways. Sir, if you're reading this book, and you survived, I have one of your teeth. It's in my scalp.

AVOIDABLE?: I can see him now, the grim figure—hovering at the foot of my bed and pointing a skeletal finger at me, as if to say, "*Soooooon.*"

AFTERMATH: I began speaking very strangely. A friend who had been skiing with me pretty much saved my life by insisting I actually see a doctor. It was a bright and sunny day and yet—no joke—I kept commenting on how cloudy and gray the skies were.

CONCUSSED?: Yes. And it turned out I had fractured my skull. It was a real "teachable moment."

#11: "Kegger Header"

TIME PERIOD: High school

INCIDENT REPORT: During an illicit teenage party held while my parents were out of town, karma visited me in the form of a concussion I sustained while jumping into a lower level of the house. My skull struck an overhang—actually shattering the plaster—and I flew into an open bathroom and landed on the cold, sweet linoleum.

AVOIDABLE?: No. I feel that the poor judgment that caused this incident can be blamed on the other, previous concussions.

AFTERMATH: I eventually crawled out of the bathroom and lay in a heap in the basement, until discovered by my saviors: drunk teenagers. My friend Dominic commented on the giant burgundy imprint of the wall stamped into my forehead, and I resumed drinking.

Sure, most of us look back on our formative years, and we shake our heads, or whatever stumps we have left, and chuckle about the stupid stuff we did, and how easily we could have died. But I have a story of how I *really* could have died. This actually took place when I was nineteen, but I was such a dumb and immature person that my "formative years" actually cover the ages of five through thirty-seven.

The manner in which I almost died is so stupid, and so potentially embarrassing for everyone involved—me, my family, the imaginary coroner I invented just for the purposes of this story[7]—that I almost don't want to talk about it. In fact, as I dictate this, I suddenly realize that I don't want to tell this story. It's dumb, it's dan-

---

[7] Her name is Dr. Jennyfer Blade, and she's also a sexy computer hacker.

gerous, and you will think less of me. All right, so it's settled—I *won't* relay this dark, compelling, and shocking event from my life within the pages of my memoir.

Oh, okay—fine. If you fold up a five-dollar bill and place it in the back dust cover of this book,[8] I will tell the story.[9] Go ahead, I'll wait. Great. Thanks. Here's the story.

I had a friend who, for the purposes of anonymity, we'll call "Pete."[10] Pete's dad was a gun aficionado. He had an entire arsenal of weapons and ammunition in a storage room. And—there's no way to say this without its sounding dumb and ridiculously misguided—we would play with the guns. We wouldn't toss them back and forth or anything, but we'd hold them, and pose with them, and maybe pretend we were in the non-subtitled parts of a John Woo movie. Yes, I know this was incredibly stupid. Have you ever met, or been, a teenage boy? Okay—then you know how fucking dumb they are.

One day, I'm hanging out at Pete's house and he shows me his World War II–era Colt .45—the same gun Tom Hanks uses to blow up the tank, win the entire war, and save Private Ryan in the movie *Saving Private Ryan*.[11] Pete kept this handgun between his box spring and mattress. I grabbed the pistol and started really ham-

---

[8] You *did* buy the hardcover version, didn't you?

[9] Audio or e-book customers, please shout your credit card info now.

[10] Hey, Cyrus Yang, I hope you don't mind if I tell this story. Don't worry—I won't use your real name.

[11] I'm aware that this is probably not how the film actually ends. But I have a policy of not watching the final minutes of movies I know are gonna bum me out. Like that movie *The Fault in Our Stars*, where—from what I understand—the girl eats magical ice cream and becomes a famous astronaut.

ming it up—waving the gun around, pointing it at imaginary targets. And then I pulled back the slide, cocked the hammer, and I put the gun in my mouth.

I started goofing around, trying to talk with a gun in my mouth. *"Mmmffggh,"* I said, really selling it. *"Mrrrmfffggle!"* At the time, I remember thinking, "Wow—Pete must think this is the most hilarious thing he's ever seen, because he's gone pale, and his mouth is just hanging open. He's so entertained, he can't even form words!"

I pulled the handgun from my mouth and glanced into the barrel—where I saw a hollow-point bullet glancing back at me. I looked at Pete and said the cleverest thing I could think of after having just put a loaded gun in my mouth. What I said was, "I just put a loaded gun in my mouth."

We were freaked out. But being dumb young men, Pete and I quickly ignored this brush with death. Looking back, I realize that this event was something that made us feel small, and scared, and— even worse—like there might be a lesson lurking inside. All terrible things to consider when you're a teenage boy.

That night, Pete and I went to see a showing of *Thelma & Louise*, which is the movie of choice after a near-death experience. And I could not stop shuddering in my seat. "Well, of course, Joel," you might be saying. "That's because *Thelma & Louise* featured the breakout role of future heartthrob Brad Pitt, an amazing screenplay by Callie Khouri, and assured direction from the legendary Ridley Scott."[12] Sure, those reasons may all have been part of it, but it might also be because, minutes earlier, *I had put a loaded gun in my*

---

[12] Sir Ridley, I am available for your next misguided *Alien* prequel. Call me!

mouth. I couldn't enjoy any part of *Thelma & Louise,* not even the end of the film, where Geena Davis and Susan Sarandon escape to safety in their magical flying car.[13]

I kept thinking about how close I came to dying. It was replaying in my mind: Pete's panicked look . . . the sight of the bullet peering up at me from the barrel . . . the sweet and smoky barbecue flavor of the gun muzzle. Seriously—the unexpectedly delicious taste of the gun itself was perhaps the most bittersweet detail.[14] You gotta try it! Go ahead, put a loaded gun in your mouth! I'll wait.

What really haunted me, in the days and weeks following my almost accidental, not-on-purpose near-suicide, is how, in that moment . . . everything could have changed.

For one, I would be dead. That's probably the most obvious change. But there are other, terrifying alternate realities that could have occurred because of a stupid, youthful prank.

For example, with me dead at age nineteen, cinema fans would have been denied my memorable performance as Roger the Boss in the 2011 hit *What's Your Number?* That role would've gone to the legendary Paul Newman, had he not passed away in 2008.

But there's more. My sons, Eddie and Isaac, would have been raised by two completely different people, because I would not have been alive to meet, fall in love with, and have unprotected sex with my lovely wife, Sarah.[15]

And most chilling of all? Pete would have been forced to sleep in the family room for at least a month, because his bedroom would

---

[13] Note to Hollywood: We want a sequel!

[14] Well, bittersweet *and* bittersmoky.

[15] Eddie and Isaac, if you're reading this footnote, it officially counts as "the talk."

have become an active crime scene. The disruption in his sleep patterns would have affected his grades. But within a few months, the trauma of the event would have passed, Pete's grades would have improved, and he would have ventured off to college, eager for a fresh start. Midway through his sophomore year, Pete would have fallen in with a radical religious sect, moved to Saudi Arabia, and changed his name to . . . *OSAMA BIN LADEN.*

It all could have happened. But it didn't—because I inadvertently chose to not accidentally kill myself.

As life-changing and life-ending as that event could have been, I try not to dwell on the memory.

But it's hard not to be reminded of that eerie day every time I stick a loaded gun in my mouth. What can I say? I just love the flavor!

SMELLS LIKE *TEAM* SPIRIT!

LYING, CHEATING, PLAYING FOOTBALL, AND STOPPING PLAYING FOOTBALL IN SEATTLE

I n many ways, growing up in Seattle wasn't any different from growing up in my birthplace of Rome, Italy,[1] except we wouldn't see the sun for months at a time, and instead of enjoying delicious pasta and gelato, everyone just ate heroin. I'm giving Seattle—and its rich history of intravenous drug use—a hard time, but I do truly love the city. As you have probably noticed, I reserve my sharpest sarcastic jabs for that which I hold most dear.[2]

I love Seattle *so much* that my Internet search engine of choice is Bing—a proud product of the Pacific Northwest's own Microsoft Corporation.[3] Don't believe me? I'm using Bing at this very moment,

---

[1] Thank you again for bringing that up.
[2] Like my dumb family. I love you, you roving band of slack-jawed freeloaders!
[3] Your book requires an update. Would you like to install now?

on my Apple MacBook Pro, to research little-known facts about my beloved hometown. Did you know that—according to Bing—Seattle is a Duwamish word that means "Including search results for 'Seattle.' Did you want results only for 'Seetle'?"

You might be saying to yourself, "Well, this 'Seattle' sounds just lovely. I would like to visit, fall in love with this wondrous place, and then move my loud, fat family there, further contributing to the city's growing traffic problems." Well, beware, potential visitors! Seattleites are notoriously protective of their city. And frankly, you would be too, if you had to endure an influx of people searching for Eddie Vedder's house in the early nineties.[4]

In fact, Seattle natives will actively lie to you to discourage you from uncovering the city's wonderful secrets.[5] My advice? Ignore the guidebooks, Yelp reviews, and any suspicious-looking Seattle resident who wants to steer you toward "all the cool, non-touristy" places. Instead, listen to me, a Seattle native and former resident, because I want to steer you toward all the cool, non-touristy places.

---

[4] Now it's just a bunch of lost-looking middle-aged guys in Mudhoney shirts.

[5] It actually never rains in Seattle. Every day is mostly sunny with a high of 74 degrees. The "it rains all the time" myth was created by the Seattle division of the Illuminati (core members: Shawn Kemp, Kenny G, and Anna Faris) to safeguard the city's rich flannel reserves.

THIS IS . . .
JOEL McHALE'S
SECRET SEATTLE!

➡ **Your trip should start here: Seattle's undiscovered gem, the Pike Place Market! This off-the-beaten-path open-air marketplace features fresh produce, meats, and key chains. And best of all—it's never crowded!**

Here's an insider tip: Visit the fish market and each of the employees will personally handle your order, flinging it back and forth over your head until you ask them to stop. Trust me, you haven't had *real* seafood until you've had it toughened by the busy, unwashed fingers of a Seattle fishmonger.

➡ **Nearby, there's a charming little coffee shop that serves up some of Seattle's best "joe."[6] You'll know it by the green-and-white logo featuring a mermaid (fellas, she's topless!).**

"Shhh—we don't want this place to go corporate!"

Tell the barista you want an iced caramel macchiato with chocolate chips, cinnamon, and extra whipped cream—hold the coffee. Now, that's a real, hard-core Seattle coffee drinker's coffee drink!

---

[6] Never refer to it as "joe." You sound like a fucking tourist.

➤ **And while the tourists are gapping at the boring wonder of the Puget Sound, take a detour to one of Seattle's truly hidden treasures, the Space Needle.**

Seattle's famed Space Needle.

Don't let the name fool you—this architectural wonder is earthbound, rising from the city to pierce the sky above, like a hypodermic ready to jab some much-needed China White into a hungry, waiting vein.[7]

➤ **Seattle is noted for its many connections to pop culture. Yes, the "Jet City"[8] has been featured in the films *Stakeout* and *Another Stakeout*, and the logo for TV's *Frasier*.**

Scene from *Frasier*.

---

[7] I *told* you we had a problem. But no, you just wanted us to keep churning out hit records. Well, that kind of pressure comes with a price!

[8] Named for the song "Jet City Woman," by that most popular of all Seattle bands, Queensrÿche.

While you're here, you'll want to visit the *real* locations from the beloved romantic comedy *Sleepless in Seattle*—like the landmark from the film's climax: the Empire State Building, located at 350 Fifth Avenue in New York City.

> ➤ **Thanks for visiting our lovely city. Now get the hell out and never return. And if you tell anyone about the gourmet food, the breathtaking snowcaps of Mount Rainier, or the citywide, open-air orgies that occur every Friday at three p.m., we will hunt you down and *end you.***

I spent my adolescent years in the suburb/landmass of Mercer Island—which is quiet, bucolic, with a population density of 3,591.6 per square mile.[9] It was a great location to go through puberty, get my driver's license, and eventually, somehow, graduate from high school.

I attended Mercer Island High School—home of the Fightin' No-Mascots, because the previous mascot, the "Tropical Warrior," was deemed offensive. Now, I'm a fairly liberal-minded guy, but I must say, as a proud Seattle native[10] of Irish-Norwegian descent, there was nothing offensive about the school's previous mascot, other than the name and associated imagery.

My high school experience was unique. Rather than being relegated to one clique—the jocks, the nerds, the preppies, the freaks, or the Judd Nelsons—I crossed all boundaries. I was on the rowing

---

[9] Thanks, Bing!

[10] Well, somebody else was there first. But we try to ignore that whenever possible.

and basketball teams, acted in school plays, and loved Talking Heads and Monty Python. I was chameleon-like—assuming different traits, hobbies, and skin textures in order to blend into any situation. Constructed out of various social groups, I was truly a high school Frankenstein.[11]

I won't sugarcoat it: I was a terrible student. But I was tall, handsome, and charismatic, so I skated by—through cheating and lying. You will notice this aspect of my personality is a trend as we get deeper into my life story. But there's a *real* reason I was a terrible student, and I will get into that later. It's touching, it's relatable, and it will make you feel bad for muttering, "What a conceited dick" when you read that earlier sentence where I bragged about being a good-looking, charming liar.

After high school, it was time to leave behind the safe haven of Mercer Island and venture forth into the larger world in search of higher education. So I bade my parents a tearful good-bye and hit the road—driving approximately ten miles north to the University of Washington.[12] It was an exciting time. Free of high school—with its strict curriculum and schedule—I was able to discover the real me: a not-studious person who frequently oversleeps.

Although I was already a social butterfly,[13] college would allow me to branch out even further. I was a white-bread kid who played sports, but I didn't want to have the standard, clichéd college experience. I longed to explore other cultures and interests different

---

[11] The only group I was *not* involved with were the people who liked to point out that it's actually "Frankenstein's monster."

[12] Don't take I-90—it's backed up right now.

[13] And, admittedly, a sexual caterpillar.

from my own. So I joined the rowing team and rushed the Theta Chi fraternity. You know—baby steps.

I'm the first to admit that competitive rowing is an incredibly stereotypical Caucasian activity. It's actually a whiter sport than the variation of water polo that uses a rolled-up Restoration Hardware catalog instead of a ball. Being on the rowing team for a Pacific Northwest college is one of the whitest things in the solar system.[14]

But I was recruited to row for the school, so I felt a certain responsibility. A vital and solemn responsibility to put on little shorts, sit in a boat with eight other guys, and row really fast. I would soon learn that the rowing team was very strict: you had to mind your oar grip, constantly work on your form, and, most challenging of all, not giggle when you heard the term "coxswain."

They also had weird hazing rituals for freshmen, like shaving your eyebrows and scalp and stuffing a pillow with the hair. No, really—they actually made people do this. There was, literally, an entire display case of rowing-team-member hair pillows. You know, like a serial killer would have. I have consulted numerous Bed Bath & Beyond employees, and they assure me this is not how the majority of commercial pillows are produced.

And once, the team captain actually screamed at me for not pushing in a chair properly. I was accused of being "insubordinate." (I assume toward the chair.) The team surrounded me, and one of them slapped me, which is way worse than being punched. Although it's less painful than a punch, it's three times as humiliating. I remember looking

---

[14] Aside from the celestial body Polaris (the "North Star"), which frequently follows The Dave Matthews Band on tour.

around, after being slapped in the face, and thinking, "Well, there are nine of them. I will have a real problem if I try to fight these guys."

So it turned out that the rowing team was—how do I put this?—a bunch of raging assholes. It turns out that I also hated being in a fraternity. There were some nice guys there, but the forced camaraderie and aggressive conformity of the whole experience just made me think of Nazi Germany. No, that's too harsh. It was more like Weimar Republic–era Germany. Also, this was the fall of 1991, and after sharing a house with dozens of other white men in their twenties, I had grown really, really tired of hearing Guns N' Roses' *Use Your Illusion I* and *II*. I needed to make a change. I committed myself to finding a group of easygoing dudes who just wanted to chill. So I walked on to the University of Washington national championship football team.

I was already athletic—I was used to weight training and had a good build from rowing, plus my abs were finely honed from suppressing laughter whenever I heard the word "coxswain." I was young, dumb, and full of competitive spirit. I was also—as I mentioned earlier—a thoroughly committed liar, so I told the football coach that I had played in high school until I was sidelined by an injury. It was a harmless little lie—that would soon cause me a great deal of ironic bodily harm.

Being in my early twenties, I fancied myself indestructible, which is, I guess, why I thought I could simply waltz onto the roster for one of the most fearsome college football teams in the country. But I did walk on—to the legendary U-Dub Huskies—and then was repeatedly carted off after being knocked unconscious.[15]

---

[15] I wasn't literally knocked out. But I prayed for the sweet release of unconsciousness on several occasions.

A walk-on is a player who, while not necessarily skilled enough to be a starter, is still valued—as human tackling meat, for both practice *and* entertainment purposes. As a walk-on tight end, I was brutalized. I was cannon fodder. They could have just used an actual tackling dummy, but then the linebackers wouldn't have had a real opponent who could move, react, and writhe in agony.

In practice, we would run "hot routes"—that's where you sprint five yards, spin around, and have a pass thrown to you. Then, a man who outweighs you by sixty pounds—in my case, All-American middle linebacker Dave Hoffman—tries to legally murder you.[16] Actually, Dave is a really nice guy and he wasn't trying to murder me. It was more like very spirited attempted manslaughter.

But I did not die,[17] and my time on the Huskies was rich and rewarding. I had committed myself to a goal—getting injured on a football field in front of an indifferent coaching staff—and I pushed my body and my will to achieve that goal. Although I never played during an actual game, I did set the team record for "number of times the wind was knocked out of a single player."

And college football led me, however indirectly, to my actual career. The team had a "skit night," where players honored the performing arts by putting on dresses, lip-synching, and doing bad impersonations of the coach. I performed in a comedy sketch as the team doctor—a man whom I had been introduced to, and reintroduced to, on several occasions—and I nailed it. My teammates were laughing and enjoying themselves—and it was all because of me. For

---

[16] This is what contact sports actually are: organized murder, with jerseys.

[17] Current score—McHale: 2; football/self-inflicted accidental gunshot wounds: ZERO!

once, my friends and peers were in hysterics, and it wasn't due to both of my eyes bleeding after a tackle. I thought to myself, "I may have something here. If I can entertain that most discerning of audiences—college athletes—then maybe I should go pro."

The team wound up going to the 1993 Rose Bowl. I got a PAC-10 football championship ring, but more important, I also gained a newfound purpose. And it wasn't to spend all my waking hours with athletic men in various states of undress. Nope, I wanted to do something manlier: acting! I walked away from sports, but the football legacy that I forged—with my own blood and sweat—speaks for itself.

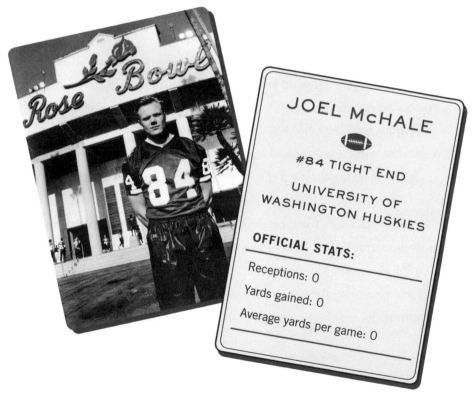

5

I WANT TO SAY
HER NAME IS . . . AMY?

A BRIEF APPRECIATION OF THE SIGNIFICANT OTHER
WHO REAPS THE BENEFITS OF MY SUCCESS

S o we've established that I was an occasionally dishonest, accident-prone young man torn between two potential careers. There was professional acting, one of the most reliable means of procuring income,[1] and my short-lived dalliance with collegiate sports.

Which one would I choose? Well, since only one of those is an actual career,[2] you receive *no points* for guessing that I chose acting. And yes, I am scoring you throughout this book. So far you have a 57 out of a possible 78. But you can get bonus points for reading all the footnotes![3]

I loved performing, and making people laugh, and okay, sure,

---

[1] In my experience, anyway. I guess for other people it can be a little tough sometimes.
[2] According to the NCAA.
[3] Just not this one, you suck-up.

wearing makeup and funny clothes and getting called by names that were not my own. It had been a part of my DNA since childhood. Whether it was the freedom of creativity or just the chance to be the center of constant attention,[4] it was official—at an early age, I had been bitten by the acting bug!

A young Joel McHale is attacked and bitten by the Acting Bug—which has the body of Daniel Day-Lewis, the six arms of Tilda Swinton, the head of Paul Giamatti, the flawless artistic instincts of Alfre Woodward, and the unfortunate facial hair of Sean Penn.

I fell in love with acting at a young age, but didn't want to go all the way until both of us were old enough.[5] I was a budding actor in

---

[4] Have I mentioned I'm the middle child?
[5] Until I was in my early twenties, and acting was 1,981 years old.

Seattle and had landed an internship on the legendary local sketch comedy show *Almost Live!*[6] So, in terms of my attraction toward performing, I had reached second base—I had acting's shirt off and was struggling with its brassiere. And that is when life threw my heart (and eventually my genitals) a curveball—in the form of the human lady love of my life.

At this point, you are probably wondering just what kind of woman could possibly be attracted to me. Well, since I have been happily married since the mid-nineties, the kind of woman attracted to me is specifically my wife. And your questioning her like that triggers the "defend loved one at all costs" part of my lizard brain, so maybe you and I should step outside, chief.[7] I've had girlfriends before—in high school and college and a couple weeks ago—but each of them has politely requested, through legal counsel, not to be included in this book.[8]

I met my future wife in college, as I was walking home from football practice. I remember each and every detail as if it happened yesterday. It was a cool September evening in 1992. Or, wait—it was 1991. Actually, it feels like it was an unseasonably warm January in 1993, but that can't be right. It's all a little bit hazy.[9]

---

[6] One notable *Almost Live!* alumnus was "Bill Nye the Science Guy," back when he was just "Bill Nye the Struggling Comedian Guy."

[7] That's right—outside of whatever airplane cabin or bathroom you're reading this book in.

[8] I assume. The restraining orders prevented me from getting close enough to ask them.

[9] Please refer back to the section in chapter 3 detailing my numerous head injuries.

SPOV—SARAH'S POINT OF VIEW: Hi, it's me, Sarah McHale— Joel's wife. Like I do in our marriage, I will appear at random intervals throughout this chapter to offer my own recollection. Or as it is commonly known, "the truth."

Sarah, stop interrupting and go wait in the car. Anyway, I remember walking home from football practice, alongside my older brother, Christopher. I recall vividly that he was there, because people kept leaning out of windows as we passed and saying, "Hey, quit shouting. We're trying to study—this is a college campus."

We passed the Kappa Alpha Theta sorority, and there was Sarah, talking with a girl who went to my high school— we'll call her "Kim O'Neill."[10] I had heard the legend of this "Sarah Williams"—how she was smart, and funny, and really attractive.

SPOV—SARAH'S POINT OF VIEW: This is all accurate. Continue.

Sarah also wouldn't date anyone. And I am a man who is drawn to a challenge. Unless it's something really, really difficult, like math—in which case, I give up pretty quickly. But I remember thinking, "This girl is

---

[10] Hi, Kim O'Neill! You helped me meet my lovely wife, so you get your own footnote. I also gave one to the kid whose gun I almost used to accidentally kill myself!

just my type: beautiful and unavailable." Which, if we're being honest, is *every* human being's type of human being.

Sarah and I had a brief but spirited conversation.

SPOV—SARAH'S POINT OF VIEW: Joel looked at me and said, "Hey. 'Sup?"

I was immediately drawn to her. There was something magical about that night—the air particles were charged, our pheromones were pinging off each other,[11] and we were all feeling a bit woozy and light-headed with true love's first blush.

SPOV—SARAH'S POINT OF VIEW: It turned out to be a gas leak at the sorority. Our house mother discovered it just in time. She saved a lot of lives that night. Anyway, here's what I remember: Joel had terrible posture. Like, *really* awful. He was hunched over like a Neanderthal. But he was also kind of handsome. And he seemed to think he was funny. Which, in and of itself, was entertaining.

I looked at this charming young woman, and I thought, "Joel, play this cool. Show her respect, treat her like a human being, and maybe eventually she'll let you touch her boob." There

---

[11] I don't know how pheromones work. Or what they are.

was a spark that day, or at least I thought there was. Sarah would later claim this was not the case.

SPOV—SARAH'S POINT OF VIEW: That was *not* the case. But he was kind of cute.

For the next couple years, Sarah and I would run into each other at various events: parties, a friend's wedding, outside of her window while she slept. I'm kidding. I didn't watch her sleep. Her bedroom was on the second floor of the sorority house, so I quickly realized that was impossible.

SPOV—SARAH'S POINT OF VIEW: I do remember thinking that he was stalking me—but in a harmless kind of way. Which is why you're hearing this story within a humorous memoir and not an eight-part Netflix documentary.

Toward the end of college, I was cast in an incredibly low-budget movie. So low-budget that the entire two-hour film was scheduled to be shot over a single weekend.[12] The movie was an independent thriller called *American Messiah*, and I landed the pivotal role of "Affordable Local Actor." In the movie, I killed the title character, which immediately typecast me as the "dickhead boss/ex-boyfriend/serial killer"—the kind of roles that would clog my future filmography.

---

[12] This is not how it's usually done. Feature-length movies usually take at least five or six days to complete. Some, like *Avatar*, can shoot for an entire week.

Sarah's brother, Richard, was working on the movie, and I found myself immediately drawn to his warmth and womanly hips. They both reminded me that I should make one last attempt to win his sister's heart. This time, I wouldn't take "No" or "Put your hands in the air and step away from the sorority house window" for an answer. I would put it all on the line and take a big risk—by calling Sarah's friend Kim and asking, "What's Sarah's deal?"

Kim was incredibly helpful. I believe her exact words were, "You don't have a chance." I just smirked, which did not play as well over the phone as I'd hoped. "Joel, are you still there?" Kim asked. I smirked again, exhaled heavily into the receiver a couple of times, and then hung up the phone.

My next call was to Sarah. I gathered my courage and asked her if she'd like to go out sometime. I must have caught her in a moment of weakness, because she relented, saying, "Sure—come on over. We can make cookies together." I hung up the phone before she could change her mind. But I would soon be crestfallen to learn that "make cookies together" was not code for "have sex."

SPOV—SARAH'S POINT OF VIEW: I found his innocence sweet and his stupidity disarming. My mom immediately put him to work moving heavy stuff around the house. And we made cookies.

I froze one of those cookies, and I take one lick every year on our wedding anniversary. This usually makes me very ill, because cookies aren't meant to last that long. But it's worth it—because that cookie symbolizes the moment that Sarah and I fell in love.

SPOV—SARAH'S POINT OF VIEW: Actually, I think we *mutually* fell in love about a year later. And I wish you would just throw away that disgusting old cookie.

I graduated from college in the summer of 1995 and parlayed my internship with *Almost Live!* into a real, honest-to-God, very low-paying acting job on the show. Prior to this mini windfall, I was so broke, I didn't even own a car. This caused some minor friction with Sarah's family, who assumed I was just using her for free rides in her sweet white Chevy Corsica.

Flush with a new job that elevated my financial status from "instant ramen for dinner" to "*brand-name* instant ramen for dinner," I figured the time had come to ask Sarah to join me in an incredibly uncertain future.

SPOV—SARAH'S POINT OF VIEW: Joel had actually asked me to marry him several times before. But he was always joking. He would just turn to me at random moments and mumble, "Hey, wanna get married?" And then he'd laugh. It's actually amazing he's made a career in comedy, since—as anyone will tell you— that is a terrible joke.

Admittedly, it is a terrible joke. Mostly because it doesn't have a proper setup, the payoff needs work, and it's not technically a joke at all. It's just teasing. But I was committed to making that terrible joke into a terrible reality. I went to a jewelry store and purchased a ring on a very aggressive payment plan.[13]

It was Christmas Day 1995, and Sarah and I were seated on the same banged-up couch where we watched *The X-Files* together every Sunday. Isn't that crazy? Who would have thought that just twenty-one years later we'd have a much nicer couch.[14]

So we were sitting on this couch, and I turned to Sarah and I said, "Hey, wanna get married?"

SPOV—SARAH'S POINT OF VIEW: I thought it was his dumb joke again, so I said, "Are you serious?"

And I replied, "As serious as the heart attack that will eventually take my life, after many happy years of being your husband." And then Sarah started to cry. I think she was touched by my proposal—and the accompanying specific imagery of my future death. She said yes.

SPOV—SARAH'S POINT OF VIEW: I was very touched. I *did* want to marry him. But I also said yes in order to get him to stop talking.

---

[13] Which I just paid off last week. Thanks, residuals from the fifth season of *Community*!

[14] And I'd also get cast in the *X-Files* reboot. I guess that's the more pertinent detail. Too late—already made it a footnote.

The following summer, we had a lovely wedding, where my brother Chris murmured a very touching toast,[15] Sarah and I signed some paperwork, and we were legally bound to each other, forever and ever. I love my wife very much. I can't believe my luck—that the beautiful, cool girl who wouldn't give me the time of day in college now wakes up next to me every morning. Usually because I'm touching her boob.

SPOV—SARAH'S POINT OF VIEW: I'm gonna step out of the book right now. I might be back later. I don't know—I have some stuff to do.

Sarah and me on our wedding day. If you squint, you can spot my dad in the background, stealing silverware.

---

[15] One which our reception overflow crowd could hear in the parking lot across the street.

6

HOW THE SAUSAGE IS MADE

PROFESSIONAL INDIGNITIES THAT MAKE MY CAREER IN THE ENTERTAINMENT INDUSTRY SEEM HONORABLE

L et's roll back a little bit. The year was 1995, and I was interning on the show *Almost Live!*, a Seattle TV institution that was often compared to *Saturday Night Live*—merely because the show featured an opening monologue, topical sketches, and celebrity impersonations, and aired on Saturday nights on NBC. Personally, I thought the comparison was a bit of a stretch.

This internship was a great training ground. I sincerely loved working on *Almost Live!* The kind, supportive people at the show gave me the opportunity to mess up—and learn—all while performing on live local television. And the experience ultimately gave me the confidence to pursue other, potentially more high-profile jobs. And as fate would have it, the offers soon came flooding in! Both of them.

The nice people at *Almost Live!* wanted to promote me to official cast member, and at the same time, I was also offered a cohosting job for a *PM Magazine*–type show[1] in Portland, Oregon.[2] I couldn't believe my luck: two job offers! I was excited but quickly calmed myself. This was a big step for my career, and I needed to think deeply in order make a solid, rational decision. So I immediately accepted both jobs. Sure, they were both full-time positions, in different cities, but I had seen enough sitcoms to know that I could make this wacky, comedic situation work in my favor. It would be simple!

During commercial breaks on *Almost Live!*, I would hop into my car[3] and drive the 174 miles to the other TV studio, in Portland. On the elevator ride up to the soundstage, I would engage the emergency stop and hastily change out of my "local sketch comedy show" clothes and into my "local newsmagazine and human-interest show" clothes. I'd part my hair in a totally different direction and rush onto the set. Then I'd pound out a cooking segment with Portland's own Chef Gil Bergstrom, throw to a commercial break, and inform the producers that I'd suddenly realized I forgot my car keys.[4] I'd jump back into my car, drive north to Seattle (switching outfits as I drove), and return to *Almost Live!* just in time for the Newt Gingrich/Spice Girls/Beanie Babies sketch.[5]

"Joel, you seem awfully flustered," the floor director would say as

---

[1] Kids, ask your grandparents.

[2] Seattle's smaller, smellier brother!

[3] I was finally able to afford the car of my dreams: a 1989 Nissan Sentra two-door, held together by two scrunchies and a Koosh ball, because it was the 1990s, you see.

[4] One of them would say, "But your keys are right there in your hand, Joel." And I'd get flustered for a moment before quickly making up a new lie, probably about having diarrhea.

[5] Again, it was the '90s.

he helped me into my Alanis Morissette wig. "Oh, it's nothing," I'd blurt, out of breath. "It's just that I lost my car keys. But everything's okay, because I found them and also"—this next part I would deliver with a knowing wink at you, the viewer—"I have diarrhea."[6]

See? I would make this work. Or *could* have made this work, if the two shows didn't immediately rescind their offers after discovering I had accepted both. This was a real learning experience for me and taught me a very grown-up lesson: it's impossible to maintain two full-time jobs, no matter how excited, hardworking, and greedy you are. I would think back on this lesson often as I rushed from the set of *The Soup* to my other full-time job on *Community*.

So within a matter of minutes, I went from juggling two jobs, to having an elaborate fantasy about juggling two jobs, to juggling zero jobs. Thankfully, the *Almost Live!* people took pity on me and again offered me a role on the show. Sorry, local Portland TV newsmagazine, whatever you were called—but it wasn't meant to be.

As a performer on *Almost Live!*, I became a local celebrity. My castmates and I were invited to events, galas, festivities, soirees, get-togethers, bacchanals, and thesaurus release parties. This was my first taste of fame, and frankly, I was frightened by how much I fucking loved it. C'mon! Free booze, free finger sandwiches, free gift bags? People treating you differently just because you play pretend on TV? I don't know why everybody doesn't do it.[7]

Anyway, I was really living the high life . . . on five hundred dollars a week. It's frighteningly easy to take advantage of a young,

---

[6] And there you have it, dear readers, the origin of my beloved catchphrase!

[7] Note to everybody: Do not do it. I have a pretty sweet setup here, and I don't need a bunch of fame- and finger-sandwich-hungry yokels messing it up for me.

hungry actor, and I was woefully underpaid. This was my first brush with the seamy underbelly of the creative life, and I didn't like the coarse feel of the seams or the fetid smell of the belly. I guess that's why it's tucked under there. Regardless, being treated unfairly by an entity I had trusted for years just proved that the old Hollywood adage was true: "That's why it's called 'Showbiz Pizza' and not 'Show*friends* Pizza.'"[8]

Actually, it turned out that *Almost Live!* wasn't purposefully underpaying me—it was the result of a simple clerical error. Being the thoroughly decent people they were and are, they quickly paid me what I was owed. (Sorry, guys. Didn't mean to be overly dramatic a few sentences ago. Just trying to manufacture some creative conflict.) I enjoyed my time as a local Seattle celebrity. But I quickly realized that if I wanted to go further—to stretch myself creatively, open up acting opportunities, and potentially get invited to fancier thesaurus release parties—I would have to keep pushing myself. I needed to get much more seriouser about my acting, and—time permitting—my grammatical skills.

I made the decision to step away from my job on *Almost Live!* I loved everything about that show. Simply getting the chance to do TV sketch comedy every week was amazing. But I knew that if I stayed too long, I'd eventually wind up with a career as the wacky

---

[8] It's also not called "Showbiz Pizza, as it was purchased and rebranded by Chuck E. Cheese's in the early nineties. This was all part of the surprisingly complex and fascinating world of the animatronic-themed pizza restaurant industry. For more on this subject, read my other book, *A Slice of Heaven: Showbiz, Chuck E. Cheese's, and the Halcyon Days of Robot Mice Selling Pizza to Children.*

traffic or weather guy on Seattle radio.[9] The time had come for me to hunker down and focus on actual, serious, nonmarketable training as a real actor.

It has been said that repeating the same action and expecting a different result is the definition of madness.[10] Now, I had always struggled with school. I had trouble focusing, I didn't seem to learn like other people, and this resulted in many very frustrating years for me. So I thought, "I know what I'll do: I'll go back to school."

But this time, I would put the skills I had perfected in high school and college—lying, being charming, being charming *while lying*—to good use, by *majoring* in them! So I reenrolled at my alma mater, the University of Washington, to pursue a master's degree in theater. Now when I lied, it couldn't really be called "lying"; it would have to be called "acting."

I threw myself into my formal acting training and soon learned how to discuss my craft, study my characters' psychological motivations, and do it all while suppressing the urge to punch myself in my newly pretentious face. We studied the "Suzuki method," which I assumed was where you shout dialogue from *The Lost Boys* while doing sick motorcycle doughnuts in a parking lot. But, nope. Instead, it was a martial arts–inspired form of theater exercise, only

---

[9] Not that there's anything wrong with being a local radio personality. I love you guys! And I'm performing this weekend at the Indian casino closest to you! Now let's give away some tickets.

[10] An oft-repeated quote that is alternately credited to Benjamin Franklin, former New Orleans Saints nose tackle Tony Elliott, and the creators of the *Air Bud* movie franchise.

way less cool than it sounds.[11] You were supposed to march a lot, then spring into dramatic poses, and recite lines from vaunted works of theater like Euripedes's *The Trojan Women*. Needless to say, I was bummed. Especially when everybody teased me about my Kiefer Sutherland wig on the first day of class.[12] For the life of me, I still don't know what the Suzuki method was supposed to do. My instructors said something about it deepening concentration or something. I don't know—I wasn't really paying attention, anyway.

There was a lot of this touchy-feely, artsy-fartsy stuff in theater school. But I approached acting in much the same way I had played football—where there is no touchy-feely stuff, the art is simply in how your body responds to challenges, and the farting is merely incidental. You can do drills all you want, but you have to actually *play* in order to improve—so I acted wherever and whenever I could.

I honed my acting skills in an ad for the Ford Aspire,[13] corporate videos for Microsoft,[14] and a Washington State Lottery commercial with legendary fitness guru Jack LaLanne. This was back when Jack was eighty-four years old and still giving people aerobic advice. He resembled a bunch of beef jerky sticks coiled together inside a unitard. And I sincerely mean that as a compliment. I don't remember how the ad agency made the connection between Jack and scratch-off lottery tickets, but I believe it had to do with how lucky he was that his arteries had not yet hardened.

I even performed a one-man show about Sylvester Stallone where

---

[11] Meaning, no ninja throwing stars.
[12] "You're eating maggots, Michael. How do they taste?"
[13] As in, "I *aspire* to someday own a much nicer car."
[14] The makers of the Zune you're reading this book on!

I analyzed his filmography—by reenacting one line of dialogue from every movie he ever made. And what I learned from that comedic exercise is that nobody, in the history of cinema, has appeared in more bad movies more successfully than Stallone. It's an incredible feat that I hope to someday top.

I graduated in 2000, with a real, honest-to-God master's degree. That's correct. I, Joel McHale, am just one step removed from being *Dr.* Joel McHale.[15] Everyone graduating from the University of Washington theater program was given the opportunity to perform in a showcase. An acting showcase is a lot like those Japanese seafood auctions you see on Travel Channel shows. Only in this case, instead of a sushi chef bellowing, "That tuna looks sufficiently marbled!" it's a bunch of talent scouts and agents. And they usually shout more about you needing to get your teeth fixed and less about your fat marbling.

My graduating class performed at two showcases—one in New York, the other in Los Angeles. I traveled first to New York City, with my other income-challenged actor buddies. I slept on the kitchen floor of a friend's tiny apartment and was awoken every twenty minutes by his cat licking my face. As a result, the night before my showcase, I had stress dreams about someone repeatedly slapping me with wet sandpaper.

The day of the showcase, my actor buddies and I went to the 2nd Ave Deli, and—in what I would quickly learn is not a traditional pre-performance ritual—we decided to pool our money and share

---

[15] Any accredited universities desperate for a commencement speaker are encouraged to contact my publicists.

the MEAT PLATTER. I capitalize "MEAT PLATTER" because it was a gigantic, delicious bucket of various cured animal pieces. This was about an hour before my showcase performance, and I thought this was a good idea.

The real problem is that my parents always told me to eat everything in front of me. I believe my mom viewed this simply as a version of "Now, don't waste your food," while my dad—being infinitely cheaper than my frugal mother—took the more strict interpretation. For him, "Eat everything in front of you" meant "Clean your plate, shove your tablemates' food into your pockets when they're not looking, and cram saltine packets into your mouth before you're forcibly removed from the restaurant." With that guiding principle etched into my soul, I looked upon whatever my friends were too shy to ingest from the MEAT PLATTER and shoved it into my mouth.[16]

Minutes later, the theater halls were packed with young actors doing their young-actor things: vocal warm-ups, turtleneck adjustments, and reflecting on whatever their parents did to drive them into acting. But I was prone on the floor, trying to pass four pounds of nitrates. I was pale and sweaty, and worst of all, I had violated the most sacrosanct of all actor laws: I had ingested solid food.

But I didn't have the time to die of a meat overdose or to picture how embarrassing the wording of that epitaph would be. I donned my Self-Important Acting Man tank top, in standard *No Exit* black,[17] and went out to strut my stuff, and hopefully not strut any stuff into my pants. Miraculously, I did not require heart defibrilla-

---

[16] Including an entire stack of beef tongue.
[17] Available at H&M! Ask the struggling actor working there to help you with sizing.

tion, nor did any of the MEAT PLATTER return to visit me. Instead, a strange serenity washed over me—the warmth that visits a person who is on the cusp of embracing their life's true purpose. Or it could have been my circulatory system trying to figure out where to stash all that sodium.

I went onstage, and rather than perform a typical, super-serious actor monologue, I did a sketch from one of my favorite shows, *The Kids in the Hall*. And people loved it: my fellow students, the assembled talent scouts and producers, everyone was overheard exclaiming, "That kid with the meat sweats has really got something!"

Next up, I took my killer showcase piece—the one certain to set me on the path to stardom—to Los Angeles, where . . . it got no reaction. The audience there was totally different than in New York—in that there was no audience. Barely anyone showed up. In New York, people had a passion and an appreciation for acting—it was considered an art form. But in Los Angeles, acting seemed to be thought of as a parlor trick—just one more way to turn a profit. So I knew where I belonged: in Los Angeles, of course.

As much as I admired stage acting, that was never my thing. I wanted to be a television and movie actor, and LA was the place for that. I also had an innate feeling that I should go to a city where it would be much more daunting for me to carve out a career. Call it a sixth sense for self-punishment. The one that I've had since I was a doe-eyed little boy playing Knife Catch with my brothers on the roof of our childhood home.

I always knew, deep down, that I had to move to Los Angeles eventually. In fact, I mentioned this to Sarah, even before I ever proposed to her. Sarah, like me, grew up in Seattle. Her family was there. She had deep roots in the city. I knew this would be a tough sell.

But I sat her down and told her that if we were to stay together, she'd have to leave Seattle so I could chase my tenuous dream of becoming a professional actor. It was a real "love me, love my extremely reckless career choice" kind of deal. She didn't even think about it. "Yeah, I know," she murmured. I can't remember if she even looked up from whatever magazine she was reading.

So my incredibly generous and occasionally distracted wife was on board. But I needed something to keep me diligent and focused, so I set a clock on my dreams: five years. If I hadn't achieved what I wanted—regular employment in the entertainment industry—in that time, then we would return to Seattle. I announced these plans, yet again, out loud to Sarah, and yet again, she murmured something supportive while not looking up from whatever she was doing.

So it was settled: we were moving to LA! Sarah had gotten a job at a graphic design house there, so she actually left Seattle before me. I bade a fond farewell to the Pacific Northwest, plugged "LA" into my new GPS system, and hit the road. And when I arrived, I immediately soaked up the local culture: the lights, the live music, the rich food that was, like the residents, a charming blend of influences from Europe and the American South. Days later, I received a panicked call from Sarah.

"Joel, where are you?"

"I'm here, in beautiful, steamy LA. Where are you?"

"What?!" she shouted. "I can't hear you over the sound of that New Orleans jazz combo in the background and *oh fiddlesticks you went to Louisiana instead*, didn't you?" (My wife never swears.)

The conversation that followed—an extended argument about the crucial differences between abbreviations and postal codes—was an important one in our marriage. But Sarah's already tenuous faith in my reading comprehension skills was deeply shaken.

So, okay—I'm not the brightest guy. But that wouldn't matter at all—not where I was headed next. I was bound for the only city in the world where intelligence is considered a liability: L-A-comma-C-A, baby. I stuffed my pockets full of all the hot gumbo I could grab and jumped in the car.

Los Angeles, here I was coming!

7

HOW THE SAUSAGE IS ALSO MADE

HIGHLIGHTS FROM MY EARLY CAREER, MY MID-EARLY CAREER, MY MID-CAREER, AND EVERYTHING IN BETWEEN

It was the year 2000. The potential Y2K crisis had come and gone without a hitch.[1] It was the twenty-first century—officially the future, which was weird because it distinctly felt, as I experienced it, more like the present. But looking back, it now doesn't seem like either of those things.

Anyway, I had just arrived in Los Angeles. Mine was truly a unique, one-of-a-kind story in the City of Angels: I was an aspiring TV and movie actor, searching for my shot at the big time. I am a pragmatic person and knew my work would be cut out for me. There had to be at least a dozen other people in the greater Los Angeles area who wanted the exact same thing that I did.

But I had an ace in the hole: a high-powered manager who could

---

[1] Will Smith's *Hitch* was still five long years away from release.

talk me up and do the moving-and-shaking necessary to get me noticed. At least, that's how I described my high school friend Jason Burns, who had moved to LA ahead of me and was trying to break into the talent management business. Years later he would shift to a more reputable part of the entertainment industry, by producing soft core pornography for the Playboy Channel. "Sure, I'll pretend to be your manager," Jason said, shrugging at me, over drinks. I was so touched that I offered to pay for my half of the bill. It was the least I could do.

I was off and running. I went on auditions, I networked, I rubbed elbows—I rubbed *anything* people wanted to have rubbed. The seasons changed, friends came and went, and Sarah and I settled in for the long haul. Although my confidence often faltered, I never gave up. It was a torturous wait, but my big break finally came, nearly two and a half months after I first moved to LA.

I landed an audition for the hit sitcom *Will & Grace*, which was great—it was not only a well-respected show but also a socially impactful one.[2] The guest role called for an actor who was both funny and over six foot seven. I was, tragically, three inches too short (or six, if I've just gotten out of a cold shower). But I had another childhood friend who would help me: lying. I summoned the wisdom that comes with a master's degree in professional lying and rushed over to a famous Hollywood starmaker: the Skechers Factory Store. I asked the kindly shopkeep for the tallest sneaker-boots he had, in a size 13. Yeah, you know what they say about a guy with big feet, baby. He has big dreams![3]

---

[2] Because it indirectly led to *The Mysteries of Laura*.
[3] And an adequate penis.

I put on my subtly thick-heeled new sneaker-boots and clomped into the audition, now physically tall enough, and nearly talented enough, to land the part—which I did, and just in time, as my ankles were noticeably buckling. It was my first real Hollywood acting job, and I was determined to soak up every last detail: the delicious chocolate-covered espresso beans on the snack table, the stunning assortment of sparkling waters, and, of course, my talented costars: the brown-haired guy, the other brown-haired guy, the one lady, and then the redhead, who I think played "Will."

The episode was directed by a genuine television legend: James "Don't Call Me 'Jimmy,' You Fucking Day Player" Burrows. He has directed episodes of such beloved TV shows as *Cheers*, *The Mary Tyler Moore Show*, *Friends*, and *Gary Unmarried*. He was a little brusque with me, which I guess is his style. In fact, he really didn't speak to me, or look in my direction at all, until I started getting laughs from the cast at the table read.

The table read is a treacherous experience for a guest actor. I didn't realize this at the time, but it's like a "secret" second audition—and if things aren't clicking, or you've spent too much time commenting on the chocolate-covered espresso beans, you can be quickly replaced. Luckily, I had no idea I was in any danger. I was loose and just messed around. So, lying got me my first big break, and my other special skill—horribly misplaced confidence—helped me keep it.

The filming of the episode went great—and best of all, I got to meet Sydney Pollack, who played the dad of one of the brown-haired guys. Sydney was the definition of a "mensch"—a word that, as an extremely Caucasian person from Seattle, I had just learned, and was throwing around like so many tchotchkes. Here was this legendary director and actor, and he was very cool to me and incredibly generous with his time. He didn't even bat an eye when the awkward, pale day player in oversized sneakers asked him to dinner. I didn't know this wasn't something people normally did—just traipse up to an Academy Award winner and shout, "Hey, Sydney Pollack, wanna get a sandwich with me?"

But I did, and to his credit, he didn't bail. Sydney had just finished acting in the Stanley Kubrick movie *Eyes Wide Shut* and had lots of crazy anecdotes—about the naked actress whose only job was to lie around for eight hours a day, and Kubrick's insistence on tons of takes, and how unbelievably tall Tom Cruise is in real life. It was a delightful evening, marred only by the fact that I never asked Mr. Pollack for professional advice. I had the chance to get advice from a true Hollywood legend, and instead I just kept asking for details about that naked actress in *Eyes Wide Shut*.

In that short meeting, Sydney Pollack—through his simple kindness—made a huge impact on the course of my career. And I like to think I made a big impression on him, since he never joined me for a meal again, or spoke to me, or cast me in any of his projects. Thank you, Sydney. You were a very nice man and I hope you enjoyed your Caesar salad with grilled chicken.

The exposure from appearing as the unforgettable, fan-favorite "tall guy" character in the sixteenth episode of the third season of *Will & Grace* finally got me some attention from semiprofessional agents. I say "semiprofessional" because they were two very interesting gentlemen: one of them smoked pot constantly, while the other gave me useful advice, like how to locate the best prostitutes in Spain. Sure, I had agents who were more preoccupied with their own specific vices than with finding me more "tall guy" roles. But the most important part of that previous sentence is this: I had agents!

And then I didn't book a TV or movie job for an entire year. My agents dropped me. I no longer had agents!

Their advice, upon kicking me to the curb, was, "Come back to us in four years, when you're bigger." They were letting me go because it was too difficult to find me acting jobs. "Go find yourself some work," they were essentially saying. "And then return, so we can profit from it. Bye!" You might think that makes no sense, but this is exactly how Hollywood works. There is no logic to it. People look at you, compliment you, say they'd love to give you a break, and then tell you to come back once someone else has given you that much-needed break. It's like a snake eating its own tail—only in this scenario, the snake is also asking itself for 10 percent of its own earnings.

With no job and dwindling prospects, I turned to a life of crime. I would roam the streets pulling innocent drivers from their cars, beating them senseless, and taking their money. It was the early 2000s, and *Grand Theft Auto III* was very popular at the time. I spent my days playing that game, going on auditions, and then returning home—to resume my life as a digital drug dealer. This was definitely not part of my five-year plan.

I had hit a low point. Even though, in reality—and I'm gonna sound like a spoiled dick for saying this—I was working constantly.

I went on tons of auditions for TV commercials, which I would regularly book. I was making decent money—the kind of money that ensures you can spend most of your free time terrorizing video game hookers.[4] People with normal jobs are probably rolling their eyes while reading this. And struggling actors aren't reading this at all, because—in a fit of jealous rage—they've just thrown the book across the room or down the aisle of the plane they're on.

But money notwithstanding, it was a frustrating time. I was auditioning just to smile and sell products—when what I really wanted to do was smile and *indirectly* sell products, by appearing in the shows that the products funded. This was not what I'd pretended to learn from acting school. So I turned inward, telling myself that if I was going to be a paid shill, I would be the greatest, most prolific shill in the history of advertising. To make it stick, I shouted this proclamation to my wife, in the middle of a vigorous lovemaking session.[5]

I committed to booking every single commercial job I could—and I had an impressive streak. I starred in an ad for Bud Light and what felt like[6] nearly two hundred commercials for Burger King. I even appeared in a commercial for a product called the Fire & Ice Grill, a brilliant, if structurally dubious, creation that combined a

---

[4] To the point that your wife comes home from her graphic design job, sees your tattered cargo shorts, and asks you if you've bathed that day.

[5] We were in the "spoon" position, as I secretly hoped my first child would become an acclaimed chef. Or silverware manufacturer.

[6] To me, and to viewers.

gas grill with an ice chest. That's right—two of nature's primordial forces, in the hands of hungry drunks.

During the production of this commercial, I was tasked with operating a prototype of the Fire & Ice Grill. You were supposed to press a lever with your foot, and the grill would gently and majestically rise into place, above the cooler. I assume this was so that when you reached for another Milwaukee's Best, you could rest your weary forehead on the searing-hot grill grates. Flawless design be damned, the thing would just not work. So the producers installed car shocks into the Fire & Ice Grill, and on the next take, it worked so well that the entire contraption shot into the air and flipped over. This prototype was a barely thought-out, incredibly dangerous device, and if you purchase one off eBay, I will be happy to autograph it for you.

Auditioning is a dehumanizing process—and that's the point. Casting directors, producers, and executives need to break you down into easily graspable traits, so they can more efficiently reject you. You can shrug it off as "just business," but that doesn't change the fact that getting passed over for an acting job can feel like a direct rebuke of, well, take your pick: your looks, your personality, your talent, your relationship with one of the show's writers who swore you'd get the part.

I quickly warmed to the process and its cruel Darwinian logic. So how did I survive several years of this shame parade? I learned a few simple, easy-to-follow tips!

JOEL McHALE'S GUIDE TO NAILING AN AUDITION

1. Be attractive
2. Look good on camera
3. Possess physical attributes that others find aesthetically pleasing
4. Any combination of the above

   . . . And it's just that easy! If you don't like this process, then you must hate art.

I went on so many auditions that I stopped being aware of what I was reading for, or even caring whether I'd get the job. For a working actor, this is what's known as "being in the zone." When you've been clubbed into complete, abject indifference, that's when the real Hollywood magic begins. Because then, you don't care—about whether you'll succeed, what others think of you, or how your dream of becoming a successful actor within five years now seems incredibly childish.

And that's when you become a truly relaxed performer and learn to weather the ups and downs of an incredibly silly business. And it's also when you look around and suddenly find yourself in front of a tattered green screen, auditioning for some show called *The "What The?!" Awards*. But that is a tale for another chapter.[7]

---

[7] The one after the next one.

8

HOW THE SAUSAGE
IS ACTUALLY MADE

SPONSORED BY

Premium Maple Pork Sausage Links™

A THOUGHTFUL EXAMINATION
OF THE ENTERTAINMENT INDUSTRY
AND SPONSORED CONTENT WITHIN MEMOIRS

Recently, I was enjoying a lovely breakfast in my well-appointed nook[1] while reading the latest financial news on my Barnes & Noble Nook.[2] Then I took my first bite of a succulent, savory, sweet and peppery Jimmy Dean© Premium Maple Pork Sausage Link™. I stopped chewing and just stared at

---

[1] It's actually an atrium.
[2] It's actually an iPad Pro.

the sausage on my plate. I was transfixed and thought, "How did this wonderful thing get made?"

And then it hit me: a craving for a second helping of delicious and nutritious breakfast sausages. And then something else hit me: the realization that the process that delivered this Jimmy Dean© Premium Maple Pork Sausage Link™ to my plate is *exactly* the same as the process that creates your favorite form of entertainment— whether it's a movie or a TV show.[3]

Without further ado, let's see how real breakfast pork is made— and how it directly parallels the entertainment industry. That's right, you've just been invited to a hard-core sausage fest. I hope you brought a bib.

THIS IS . . .

JOEL McHALE'S VISIT TO THE SAUSAGE FACTORY!

Step 1: SLAUGHTER—Don't Be Scared, There's Still "Laughter" in That Word!

Meat has to come from somewhere, folks. And in the sausage-making process—just like in Hollywood—that meat comes from living things.[4]

---

[3] But not a book. Those are carefully made by true artists.
[4] Many of them originally from the Midwest.

These raw materials are hacked from the bone, collected, and then arranged in piles—a messy process, but one that is necessary. You can't make an omelet without breaking some eggs, and you can't make the sausage next to that omelet, or the movie you're half watching while eating them both, without slaughtering swine and culling the herd of wannabe actors, writers, directors, and crafts-people.

So that's why they refer to it as a cattle call!

Step 2: GRINDING AND MIXING—Here Come the Chemicals!

Now that you've got the piles of sinew and flesh that will form your final product, it's time to make them more palatable. Shove that meat into an industrial machine that will leave the resulting mass pliable enough to accept whatever comes next. Fat will blend with tendon, insufferable actor will mix with hipster director, and before long, the salty aroma of collaboration will fill your nostrils! . . . But only if you include the right mixture of additives (prescription medication) and spices (the harder stuff).

FUN FACT: In the entertainment industry, we actually have an *award* for Mixing! Of course, we also have one for Sound Effects Editing, which seems like the same thing but totally isn't.

Hoo-boy! Smells like *hit* in here!

Step 3: CUTTING—The Fun Kind, Not the Overly Dramatic Teenage Girl Kind

Now it's starting to look like sausage and/or something you'd binge-watch on Hulu! Sure, the product already has the flavor and aroma of sausage, and the consumer *could* enjoy it in this form—but not enough people have touched it yet. So we need *lots* more hands extruding and reshaping the sausage, or just giving helpful notes about how it should be changed. Remember: All opinions are valid—even from people who've never made or actually eaten sausage!

"We're 'not loving' the whole sausage thing. Just a thought-starter, but can we rethink and make this smarter?"

Step 4: **EMULSIFYING AND STUFFING**—My Bologna *Used* to Have a First Name

Now it's time to get the product into a preapproved shape, so everyone can just go home. There are only three basic varieties of sausage: links, patties, and network sitcoms. Everything must fit into one of these categories before it goes out the door. Remember: Attempting to make a new kind of sausage is risky *and* scary!

My sausage is great—try it every Thursday at 8:30/7:30 Central on CBS![5]

---

[5] As of this printing.

Step 5: LINKING—Post Photos of Your Sausage on the Internet

We're almost there. Now it's time to shape, twist, and package our product for a hungry public. This is where the formers, linkers, and "social influencers" come into play. Their job is to take a lifeless tube of meat and mention it so incessantly that people just gotta have that tube in their mouths, hands, and DVR queues.

Now that's what I call a *hot link!*

And that's the process![6] I want to thank the good people at Jimmy Dean Sausage; their parent company, Hillshire Brands; and *their* parent company, Tyson Foods, for their cooperation and openheartedness. Speaking of open-heart, those folks were nice enough to provide several pounds of raw pork for me to take home. And I plan on eating it tonight, while I and my loved ones curl up to watch the deleted scenes from the Blu-ray release of *Transformers: Dark of the Moon*. Until next time, I'll see *you* . . . in the sausage aisle!

---

[6] Excluding the people who physically move the product and operate the machinery used to make it. But frankly, we don't pay attention to them until they threaten to strike.

CLIP SHOWS, SITCOMS, AND SITCOMS ON THE INTERNET

MY "CAREER" "IN" "TELEVISION"

I was acting in commercials, selling the poop out of light beer and fresh, flame-grilled Whoppers,[1] which was fine enough. But my dream of getting paid to be funny, or to cry on cue, or to have fake sex with people on camera, was quickly evaporating.

My friend Jason Burns was moving up the ranks as a Hollywood agent. I knew he'd successfully made the transition to the big time when he wound up at a large talent agency and then informed me he could not bring me on as a client. It wasn't Jason's fault.[2] Career-wise, I was nowhere. But I would soon wind up at an altogether different kind of nowhere!

E! Entertainment Television, at the time, was located across the street from the La Brea Tar Pits. As accurately depicted in the prescient 1997 documentary *Volcano*, the tar pits are a geological

---

[1] Note to Burger King corporate: My routing number is 594911-09672.
[2] Jason is a thoroughly decent guy, and we are still very good friends. In fact, he now runs my production company, so we talk at least once a year.

wonder that bubbles over with black sludge, noxious fumes, and molten lava, in the heart of Los Angeles's Miracle Mile. The centerpiece
attraction is a massive pool of primordial ooze, where a replica of a
woolly mammoth struggles in vain to free itself from the quagmire
that will claim its life. Statues of the beast's mate and offspring watch
helplessly from the shore. So, yeah, E! is across the street from this.

It was January 2004 and I had an audition there. Being on the
top-secret casting-director list of "tallish guys who've guested on a
couple of sitcoms" meant that I went on dozens of this kind of audition, every week. I walked in, they turned on a video camera, and
then I recited my name and the contact information for whatever
Latvian child actor agency had agreed to represent me at the time.
It was a typical audition—after I read the lines, the producers and
casting people had me sign some releases, took hundreds of photos
of my naked body, and then thanked me for my time.

And then I got a "callback"[3] for the project, which now had the
poetic title of *The "What The?!" Awards*. Some enterprising[4] executive at E! had noticed the rise of reality television and decided to
revamp the network's dormant franchise *Talk Soup*. This was during the early days of reality TV, where what had started with *Survi-
vor* quickly morphed into a nightmarish new genre that included
shows like *The Swan*, *The Mole*, and *The Apprentice*. The only thing
television programmers weren't showing was The Restraint. So
there was a lot of insane stuff out there, and E! was looking for a
smarmy dick to comment on all of it. Deep down, I knew *I* could be

---

[3] Industry jargon for getting "called back."
[4] Industry jargon for "desperate."

that smarmy dick.[5] E! seemed confident, too—I only had to go through an additional seven auditions before they finally gave up and hired me. And the rest . . . is history. Which I will now exhaustively recount.

I had done it! I finally had a job on national television, and just weeks shy of the expiration date on my five-year career-hopes-and-dreams detonation countdown. "Whew," I thought, "*that* was close." I wiped the sweat from my brow, snipped the blue wire on my bomb vest, and strolled into the E! offices.

The show had been retitled *The Soup*, which we can all agree is a slightly better—if somehow even less descriptive—name. This freed up *The "What The?!" Awards* to be used as the name of a TV special that counted down the worst show titles in television history. I just want to reiterate: I hosted a show called *The Soup*. I never hosted *Talk Soup*. *Talk Soup* went off the air in 2002. I am just pointing this out because everyone—journalists, viewers, even my own family—still insists that I hosted a show called *Talk Soup*. Do you hear that, Museum of Television & Radio? I want the plaque on my nine-foot-tall bronze statue to have the correct credits.

The Soup was indeed a reboot/reimagining/distant cousin of *Talk Soup*, a show originally hosted by Greg Kinnear. And this was a fact I clung to in the early days: if Greg Kinnear could parlay a basic-cable hosting job into a successful acting career, then maybe this guy[6] could, too.

The Soup showcased all the insane garbage from reality TV,

---

[5] *That Smarmy Dick!* was the working title of the book you are now reading.
[6] I'm smiling and pointing into a mirror right now.

which meant that I and the show's writers and producers had to comb through hours of regular garbage just to find the most appealing chunks of garbage.[7] So I took it seriously, and I was there every day—in that office across from a plaster woolly mammoth eternally drowning in tar—to document that garbage.

I had performed my share of improv comedy back in Seattle, but I had never been a stand-up-in-front-of-people-by-yourself-and-tell-jokes guy. So I approached my hosting duties like any other acting job: in this case, I was merely *playing* the role of "Joel McHale, host of *The Soup*." Like the true Method actor I am, I stayed in character, insisting that everyone in my personal life refer to me as "Joel" and also act as though I had a job hosting a weekly pop culture comedy show.[8]

The one thing I had not counted on—with my new task of reading a half hour of jokes every week—was all the reading that was involved. This will stun those of you who believe that "the guy from *Talk Soup* made all those jokes up on the fly," but those lines were written by myself and the other writers, and then compiled into a magical television device that prompted me to read them. It's called a *teleprompter*, and during the first season of *The Soup*, it was my mortal fucking enemy. The teleprompter projects the script onto the camera lens, so that while I appear to be staring at you,[9] I am actually trying to remember how to pronounce "Probst."

---

[7] The other working title for this book was *An Appealing Chunk of Garbage*.

[8] Daniel Day-Lewis used this same technique when he played a clip show host in *My Left Foot*.

[9] And for the last time—no, I cannot actually see you through your TV screen. Except for *you*, Matt Anderson of Coral Springs, Florida, you sick bastard.

I'm not what you would call "a big reader," or "a reader." I haven't even read *this* book.[10] So when I first had to read the quickly scrolling lines of the teleprompter, it was a disaster. *The Soup* was a twenty-two-minute show with no actual set, no camera movement, and—at least at the outset—no audience,[11] and yet the tapings of those first episodes sometimes ran four hours long. I could not get through a few sentences without messing up. The floor director, Tom McNamara,[12] would shout, "Bust!" whenever I'd misread something, and I heard it so many times that I still have a Pavlovian response to that word—meaning I crave one of the liver treats the producers would use to reward me.

On "the set" of *The Soup,* making pointed jokes about the artifice of
pop culture while standing in front of a wrinkled green curtain.

---

[10] But I'm really enjoying it so far. I hope the main character doesn't die at the end.
[11] Either in the studio or at home.
[12] The loudest voice you'd hear laughing during the show, either in the studio or at home.

My reading/speaking skills weren't the only challenge facing *The Soup*. At the time, E! had a split personality. On one hand, they were still very much the celebrity-worshiping network that, in the nineties, had breathlessly chronicled the opening of every Planet Hollywood location.[13] But on the other hand, they had put a satirical comedy show on the air. There were people at E! who really didn't like *The Soup*, or me, or—I assume—laughter of any kind. So those early days were filled with a lot of executive handwringing. They were worried that some celebrities might be offended by the show's jokes, and as a result, refuse to speak to E! at the red-carpet opening of the Planet Hollywood in Gurnee, Illinois.[14] There were—and I'm not exaggerating—network notes admonishing us to change Jessica Simpson punch lines so they would instead target Tito Jackson. On top of all that, my job was soon in jeopardy. During this time, certain executives were looking for any way to minimize or replace me. They tried adding a panel of comedians, guest correspondents, and anything else that meant "less of this Joel guy whom we hired to be the face of this show that we're not sure we like."

The Soup was embattled in its early days, but the show was cheap enough, and got decent enough ratings, to survive. Under the leadership of head writer and executive producer K. P. Anderson, the show found its unique voice—and I made peace with my archnemesis, the teleprompter.[15] The culture of celebrity worship and reality television—and the eventual biblical End Times brought on

---

[13] Even the one in Guam.

[14] Now a Rainforest Cafe, which oddly still displays the Pittsburgh police cap worn by Bruce Willis in *Striking Distance*.

[15] Our families now vacation together.

by both—had taken hold, and *The Soup* was riding that wave of fetid garbage-water to basic-cable glory. I remember assuming, at the time, that reality TV would eventually wear out its welcome and that our show would no longer be needed. Then a young woman made a sex tape with the brother of pop star Brandy, became famous, and brought her entire family along with her.

There was an ominous boom and the distinct whiff of sulfur, and suddenly we were surrounded by Kardashians. E! green-lighted *Keeping Up with the Kardashians*, and the show was an immediate hit. The title itself—like many of the family's pants—is a stretch, since uninteresting people who spend all of their time lounging on overstuffed couches and checking their phones are not very challenging to *keep up with*.

E! was now actively producing the same kind of crap that I openly mocked every week. This put me, and the rest of the *Soup* staff, in an awkward position. Should we display corporate fealty and comedic restraint by finding more complex targets for our skewering? Or should we gaze upon the succulent morsels laid out, banquet-style, by this oddly popular family, tie metaphorical napkins around our necks, and dive in? It took us about three seconds to decide.

By my own admission, and very lax personal moral standards, *The Soup* was often merciless. I mocked the Kardashian family, their show, and the network that put it on the air (which was also putting *me* on the air). I should point out that the Kardashians were—for the most part—pretty gracious about the constant, well-deserved mockery. I guess making millions of dollars to sit on a couch and check your phone will do that for your self-esteem. But there was one exception: I made former Olympic athlete turned professional Kardashian dingleberry Bruce Jenner very upset. So upset, in fact, that he was forced to change his name and has all but disappeared. I haven't heard anything from that guy in a long time. I guess some dudes just don't like the limelight.

The Soup came to an end in 2015, but it had already done so much for my bank account. And also my life and career, I guess. In fact, hosting that show led to the source of even more income. And also a beloved, acclaimed sitcom, I guess.

They said they need a smarmy dick," my agent told me, describing the casting process for a new NBC sitcom, *Community*. "So we've already sent them your name and measurements." The creator of the show, Dan Harmon, wanted someone who could play a sarcastic, arrogant, self-obsessed character, and upon the recommendation of a girlfriend who'd seen *The Soup*, he turned to me. I was honored. I had already been playing a sarcastic, arrogant, self-obsessed person for several years on *The Soup*, as well as for the thirty-three years prior to that. Now I would just need to adjust to a different character name, a better wardrobe, and—since this was a network TV show—much higher pay. It would be difficult, but I was certain I could rise to the challenge.

But there would be other wrinkles—for one, I still had that other full-time job, *The Soup*. And filming a complex, dialogue-heavy sitcom meant a second full-time job. In the past—as you've seen—I would have been forced to pick between the two. But that was before I had a small army of agents who could negotiate a schedule that allowed me to do everything I wanted![16] This would be an amazing exercise in both creativity and sleep deprivation.

I was so excited to be cast on *Community*. It was one of the funniest sitcom scripts I'd ever read,[17] and I threw myself into the show with an uncharacteristic amount of sincerity. *Community* premiered in the fall of 2009. And while critics didn't like us at first—"It's just goofy pop culture references!" they cried—many soon changed their opinions. I think some critics were just jumping on the bandwagon, which had been built by *Community*'s delightfully obsessive fans. "It's just goofy pop culture references!" the fans cried.

Initially, *Community* did pretty well in the ratings,[18] so the network rewarded us with a schedule move—opposite *The Big Bang Theory*, also known as "one of the most popular sitcoms in the history of television, bazinga." We faced off against that behemoth like David challenging Goliath. And just like David, we were absolutely destroyed and left for dead on Noah's ark.[19] The network executives said they loved the show, but *Community* always received very little promotional support. When they moved us to Thursdays at eight p.m., the NBC people kept trying to get us excited by saying, "It's the *Friends* time slot! We gave you the *Friends* time slot! Bazinga!" What they didn't mention is that it was also, very recently, the *Joey* time slot.

---

[16] Except see my family.

[17] Even funnier than that one where the fat guy has an attractive wife.

[18] As part of NBC's legendary "Might-See TV" lineup.

[19] Yes, I go to church and my brother is a priest. I just don't pay attention to anything either of them tell me.

Time slots no longer really mattered, since television viewers were finally realizing that, thanks to DVRs—and to a lesser extent, their own free will—they didn't have to watch television shows when they actually aired.[20] This, in turn, made people realize that they never really had to watch anything at all. Which is a very dangerous thing for the television industry, in general. This played havoc with the traditional ratings system, and many shows—especially ones that did entire homages to *My Dinner with Andre*—suffered. Of course, everything I've just described could also be applied to *The Big Bang Theory*, which, as mentioned earlier, was the most popular sitcom on TV. So take all of my excuses with a grain of salt.

On the set of *Community* in 2009, or 2012, or maybe none of it ever really happened. I was exhausted most of the time.

---

[20] If you still have unwatched *Community* episodes on your DVR, just know that *you* killed Magnitude.

Nevertheless, *Community* was a beautiful, strange bird—beloved by a passionate few, misunderstood by many, and, like all strange birds, eventually chased into another yard.[21]

Community was a dream job, and I'm not just saying that because my work schedule between the years of 2009 and 2015 left me in a permanent fugue state. I made hilarious, unique television alongside some amazing people, many of whom I'm certain I did not merely hallucinate due to severe exhaustion.

There was Gillian Jacobs, a real-deal graduate of the Juilliard School. Gillian can act your socks off, especially in a scene where her character has telekinetic sock-removing powers.[22] Gillian is an amazingly dedicated performer, and I also made out with her way more than I did with anybody else on the show. So there's that.

And then there's Danny Pudi, the nicest man I've ever met. He originally hails from Chicago, and like all Chicagoans, Danny is skinny and half-Indian and absolutely hilarious. He played Abed, the character who was the soul of *Community*. Like the show itself, Abed was odd, endearing, and ultimately not embraced by the television viewing public at large.

Yvette Nicole Brown is an accomplished comedic actress who constantly added newer, crazier facets to the character of Shirley. Also, Yvette was on Twitter more than a Russian spambot. We worked very odd, long hours on *Community*, and Yvette would often complain of exhaustion. Then I'd go back and look at her Twitter

---

[21] A yard that was once Yahoo! Screen and is now an empty lot where feral cats mate.
[22] Just like Scott Baio in *Zapped!* Hey, the critics were right, this show really *was* nothing but goofy pop culture references!

feed—to see that she was replying to people[23] well into the early morning hours. Dedication to her fans, or just a bizarre, social-media-caused form of insomnia? You be the judge!

Jim Rash, who played Dean Pelton, is one of the most inspired improvisational actors I've ever seen. He is a genuinely warm and generous human being, an accomplished director, Academy Award–winning writer, and never casts me in anything. One time, while accompanying my wife and me on a treacherous hike to the top of Mount Rainier, Jim attempted to apply aerosol sunblock, which was then accidentally inhaled by our guides, forcing them to abandon us, probably to die. "I don't know what the big deal is," Jim kept repeating as we slunk back down the mountain, our deposits long gone. You owe me three hundred bucks, Jim. That was *very* expensive sunblock.

Then there's the quiet and reserved Ken Jeong, who is much nicer than his bizarre character Ben Chang.[24] Before he started a career in comedy, Ken was an actual doctor—so he could provide medical advice ("You're taking too much Ambien, Joel") and even secret prescriptions ("No, I won't get you *more* Ambien. No one must ever know that I got it for you!"). Ken appeared totally nude in the movie *The Hangover*, and I like to think that someone went to see it, only to realize, "Hey, that's our former family doctor. And hey, that's his penis."[25]

Donald Glover had been a writer on *30 Rock* and is a talented musician and a hilarious stand-up comedian. He even performed at

---

[23] Probably Russian spambots.

[24] Although similarly prone to violent rages.

[25] Fans can still see them both, every week, on the hit ABC sitcom *Dr. Ken's Penis*.

Carnegie Hall.[26] He is an incredibly funny and giving costar who even supported me when I abruptly left *Community* for my first love, hip-hop. Thank you for that, Donald. I will never forget it.

Alison Brie is a thoroughly decent human being, a very talented actress, and a cherished source of *Mad Men* anecdotes.[27] Alison is a sophisticated, multilayered performer, which explains why her character often appeared in low-cut sweaters. Once, we took a photo of Alison's cleavage and then another photo of my butt crack. We posted them side by side on Twitter, just to see if people could tell them apart. And nobody could. I guess my upper ass cleavage was just tan and womanly enough to resemble her Brie cleavage. It fooled everyone—including Brian Williams, whose erroneous report on Cleavage-gate cost him his *NBC Nightly News* anchor job.

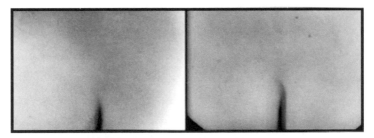

Boob or Butt? (Which is also the name of the game show that eventually replaced *Community* on the NBC schedule.)

But you didn't come here for stories about Alison Brie's cleavage.[28] No, you turned to this chapter—as you stand in the airport

---

[26] Opening for *me*. Thank you for bringing that up.
[27] All those cigarettes? Completely computer generated!
[28] Well, not *only* for that.

bookstore[29]—to read stories about something that is also legendary and scary to be in the same room with: Cornelius "Chevy" Chase.

Everyone thinks Chevy is crazy. But he's not.

He's a lunatic.

Let me preface everything I'm about to say with this: I grew up in the seventies and eighties, and I idolized Chevy Chase. *Saturday Night Live. Vacation. Caddyshack. Fletch.* What unifies them all? Yes, any male over the age of thirty-five will incessantly quote them after they've had two beers, but also, they starred Chevy Chase. The man could do no wrong—he was cool, and handsome, and funny. I'm not being sarcastic. Go watch the opening ten minutes of *Seems Like Old Times*, and you'll see a comic actor at the top of his game.

Chevy was cast as Pierce Hawthorne on *Community*. We were all excited to work with him, but Chevy was toting around some baggage.[30] He had a reputation for being difficult. I knew about this going in, but I still couldn't wait to perform alongside one of my comedy idols. When we started work on *Community*, it quickly became apparent that Chevy was not happy on the show. I don't know what he was specifically upset about but I have some theories. Now, I don't want to be an armchair psychologist here, so I'm gonna move over to this futon instead. One second.

Ah, much better. Here's how I see it: Chevy achieved great success and fame as a handsome, cool, self-assured, sarcastic guy. Take

---

[29] Just buy the thing, you deadbeat.

[30] And I don't just mean that *Oh Heavenly Dog* tote bag he carries everywhere.

it from me: that's an incredibly hard act to keep up. I can't even imagine what it's like after thirty years (and thanks to my drinking habits, I will never have to find out). On *Community*, I was the tall, sarcastic, and—okay, I'll say it—stunningly good-looking guy. Let's face it: I had been cast in the classic "Chevy Chase role." This was probably very difficult for Chevy to come to grips with. It's right there in his catchphrase, "I'm Chevy Chase, and *you're not.*"

Chevy was indeed difficult. And, not surprisingly, he often zeroed in on me. Chevy would try to "roughhouse," when it was abundantly clear that he actually just wanted to fight me. Chevy would approach me on set and say, "C'mon, boy, put up your fists." He claimed to be a Golden Gloves boxer.[31] It was all a little too aggressive to be construed as playful. He would egg me on and punch my shoulder, and I felt I had to do something.

So I'd grab his arm and bend his hand down so that it touched his wrist. Chevy would fall to his knees and ask me to stop. And then everyone on set would look at me accusingly and yell, "What the fuck, Joel?! He's old!" And Chevy would shout from the floor, "They're right! I'm old!"

In one *Community* episode, Chevy's character is teaching my character how to box. Chevy is wearing training mitts, and in the scene, I'm sparring and lightly tapping them. They call "cut" after the first take, and Chevy immediately starts chiding me:

"You're not hitting me hard enough! You gotta *hit* me!"

I replied, as calmly as I could, "That's right, Chevy. I'm not hit-

---

[31] He's not. He's Clark Griswold.

ting you very hard. Because I'm *pretending* to punch your hands, just like I'm also *pretending* to be a lawyer. And we're not actually attending a community college—this is a fake building that someone built inside of a soundstage on the Paramount lot. Look! This room has no ceiling! Because it's *all pretend*." Then Chevy called me a pussy, and again demanded, "You gotta *hit* me!" I replied, "Fine— I'll give you a left jab into your mitt." On the next take, I did just that, and dislocated Chevy's shoulder. Once again, everyone yelled at me: "Joel, what are you DOING?!"

But it wasn't just mild physical harassment. Chevy would often blurt out crazy things. One time, I referred to a close friend of mine as "the funniest guy in the world." Chevy immediately responded, "*I'M* the funniest guy in the world. *Time Magazine* said so."

To which I replied, "Yes, Chevy. But that article was published in 1975.[32] Now it's 2011, we've been here for hours listening to you complain about your dialogue, and I just want to get home and see my kids."

Oh, here's another fun one. In an effort, I think, to jokingly flatter an actress on the show, Chevy actually said, "I want to kill you and then rape you." Which, in his defense, is the most thoughtful order in which to do those things—but still. She replied, "Well, at least I'd be dead." I get it—Chevy was trying to make a purposefully tacky, over-the-top joke. But something was just off. Everything he said had a weird edge of menace.

Chevy wouldn't dance on camera because he didn't want to "look gay." This may help explain the few musical scenes in *¡Three Amigos!*,

---

[32] In *New York Magazine*, I checked and everything.

where Chevy barely moves while Steve Martin and Martin Short sing and dance like comic geniuses.[33]

During breaks in filming on *Community*, Chevy would occasionally bellow, "I can still get erections!" which is weird, because we rarely asked him about his erections. He said this phrase often enough that it became a line of dialogue in the *Community* Dungeons & Dragons episode. Chevy complained about his character being mean and offensive, which is fascinating, since Pierce Hawthorne was conceived to be a *nicer* version of Chevy.

His frustration over how his character was written led to what was easily the worst Chevy-related incident in *Community* history. We were shooting an episode where Pierce is confronted about his racism. Chevy was bristling at how the scene was written and picked the worst possible way to express his anger. He said, in frustration, "Well, if my character is this much of a racist, then why don't I just put Donald and Yvette on my knees and call them [see footnote[34]]!" I was actually the only person who heard this . . . the first time he said it. Having gone unnoticed, Chevy decided to double down, so he *repeated* what he'd said—even louder. The room fell silent. And I announced, "We've officially reached DEFCON ONE," because I like to be helpful. Chevy stormed out, and, inexplicably, headed straight to makeup and wardrobe for his next scene.

And here's where it gets even more bizarre.

---

[33] Totally gay comic geniuses.

[34] Chevy used a word that is incredibly offensive and racially charged. In fact, this word has been reappropriated by the black community for the express purpose of stripping it of its power, so that the word can be more effectively used by Quentin Tarantino.

In his next scene, Pierce was supposed to be explaining how he wasn't racist—but doing so while wearing stereotypically offensive black and Latino hand puppets. You know, the kind of subtle, nuanced sociopolitical commentary that *Community* is known for. Well, that, and those paintball episodes.

Chevy, evidently, was still stewing about the earlier events. So he burst back onto set, screaming at the rest of the cast. "You've ruined my career! I'm NOT A RACIST!" he bellowed, waving mini-sombrero-and-Afro-adorned hands wildly. We calmly asked what he meant. "It's all over the Internet!" Chevy replied before once again storming out of the room. We all immediately checked our phones, and there was nothing about this anywhere. Probably since it had literally just happened.[35]

My time alongside Chevy was alternately aggravating, bizarre, and disappointing. But it was also very illuminating. Because of my Chevy experience, I am thankful for the luck and opportunities that have graced my career, I am respectful of my costars, and I very rarely shout racial epithets anymore.[36]

And here's another thing I learned: celebrities, when startled,[37] will close ranks very quickly. Once the stories of Chevy began to circulate, I didn't feel the need to be so tight-lipped about his behavior. These were interesting tales about a compellingly eccentric man, and as such, I thought they'd make entertaining talk show anecdotes. David Letterman did not seem to agree.

I appeared on Letterman's *Late Show* in the midst of the

---

[35] And because most social media sites have filters that block hate speech.
[36] Unless I'm forced to work with filthy, devious Swedes.
[37] By a car backfiring or a paternity suit.

Community/Chevy tumult,[38] and the subject of the on-set strife arose during my pre-interview. A pre-interview is where a show producer asks you what you want to talk about, preps you on some conversation points, and then Dave ignores all that, and asks whatever he wants. During my pre-interview, they wanted to know, "Will you talk about Chevy?" My standard operating procedure with any interview is to answer whatever is asked of me, as truthfully as possible. It really annoys the shit out of my publicists. So I told the *Late Show* staffers that, sure, I would talk about whatever.

During the actual interview, Letterman asked me about Chevy—and I was probably a little too condescending (and my Chevy impersonation a bit too doddering) for his tastes. Not only did Dave not really play along, but he remarked, "Now, I've known Chevy for a very long time, and he's always been nothing but nice to me and my family." And then Letterman asked Paul Shaffer—who I suddenly remembered had worked with Chevy on *Saturday Night Live*—if his experiences were the same. "Absolutely," purred Paul, and I realized I was barking up the wrong showbiz anecdote tree.

So I softened my approach a bit—agreeing that Chevy is a legend and all that . . . while pointing out that he also enjoyed trying to fight me. Yes, I busted out the timeless defense of "Hey, Fletch would often attempt to physically assault me every morning," which seemed to win back Dave. And my story also subtly reminded Letterman that I had no compunction about injuring comedy legends who are over the age of 65.

---

[38] Somewhere, there's a community Chevrolet dealership that had to turn off its Google Alerts in early 2010.

I don't take issue with Letterman—it was his show, and he was free to defend any person he wanted, even ones who were coincidentally similar to him in age, race, and industry stature. David Letterman is another of my comedy heroes, and as much as I may have seemed like a smug prick to him, he did invite me back on his show two more times. And he never, ever stuck to the pre-interview notes—which I both admire and am still terrified by.

Honestly, that Letterman interview displayed something refreshing—that there was still some loyalty in the entertainment industry. And I hope, when I inevitably turn into a bitter, racist, older comic actor, and one of my young, hot-shit costars goes on *Conan* to tell unflattering anecdotes about me, that Conan does the right thing and puts that snide little bastard in his place. Because, look—I didn't appear in commercials for the fucking Fire & Ice Grill just to take crap from some young punk. I'm Joel McHale, and—just statistically speaking—you're (probably) not.

'm in Vancouver, staring up at the landing gears of a fake spacecraft that, alone, must have cost as much as an entire episode of *Community*.[39] I turn to the obnoxiously handsome man next to me, to ask if they ever had a spaceship that big on Showtime's *Californication*.

"You asked me that yesterday, and while I was explaining what

---

[39] Okay, half an episode. I have expensive tastes in Italian shoes that never appear on-camera.

that show is actually about, you got distracted by the sign for a Canadian McDonald's," David Duchovny murmurs in reply. I shouted back, probably a little too loud, "That's 'cause there was a little maple leaf on it, Davey!"

It's the summer of 2015, and I am—to my delight and surprise—on the set of the *X-Files* miniseries reboot thing. One of its stars has just requested that I not call him "Davey." Or "Duchovs." Or "Double-D."

"Please," he implored, his chestnut-colored eyes flickering and his mouth never once moving as he spoke. "Can we just talk about sports? You're a very strange person, and I don't want to accidentally learn anything about you." So we did, and he didn't have to.

I am, honestly, a huge *X-Files* fan. And getting cast in the reboot was a dream come true—especially since the sixth season of *Community* had recently contributed to the downfall of an Internet giant's entire video streaming service, and I like to keep busy. This was really exciting. I had reached the point in my career where my very presence could possibly be blamed for ruining beloved, long-running franchises. I had finally made it! There I was, pretending to talk to Mulder and Scully—and there were Double-D and Gillian "G-Dawg" Anderson, pretending to talk to me in between takes.[40]

The Canadian crew on *The X-Files* was so incredibly polite that it was often difficult to tell when things were really important. On

---

[40] Actual quote from Gillian Anderson, to a journalist: "Joel just talked and talked and talked." She's a super lady, and very adept at Taser use.

American shows, someone in a headset just barges into your trailer, grabs you by your most easily graspable appendage, and drags you to set, hissing, "You're supposed to be in your soiled-diaper costume, but instead you look unprepared and unprofessional!" In Canada, the crew behaved totally different.

On *The X-Files*, I would be seated in my trailer with Duchovs's latest hilarious "Get away from me" joke still echoing in my head. A set assistant would softly rap on the door and then peek inside to sweetly say, "Hey, so, uh, Joel? You know, whenever you want, if you're ready, they can have you in makeup." I'd mumble back my usual reply: "Great. Great great great," and the nice Canuck crew person would leave. Then, five minutes later, another soft knock. "Yeah, so, Joel? They really need you on set. You know, now, or whenever you can do it. Now would be great, since we're *aboot* a half hour behind." I was late and didn't even know it, because the excessively polite Canadian couldn't bring himself to tell me. This probably explains why most Canadian TV shows are only three minutes long and feature characters constantly entering scenes too late.[41]

I was cast as a conservative radio host on *The X-Files* and had tons of dialogue to memorize. Remember that time, earlier in this book . . . uh . . . thingy, where I said I'm not much of a reader? Well, lots of dialogue means lots of reading, and I was really struggling with it. Frankly, I was freaking out. I even told the show's creator,

---

[41] "Tonight, on a new episode of the CBC's *So Sorry*, Gareth arrives late to his own father's funeral."

Chris Carter, to fire me—which was an insane thing for me to say, because that would have meant a loss of money. At one point, I did not think I'd get through it—all that dense dialogue, the hot lights, the Canadian crew staring at me with their sweet, coal-black cow's eyes, silently mouthing, *"You're doin' great, eh!"* But get through it I did, and I have my own determination, and cue cards, and training to thank for it.

Community had incredible, rabid fans, but I've never seen anything like the set of *The X-Files*. We'd be standing there—me, DaDu, and Gill Pickles—trying to say lines while, across the street, hundreds of fans shouted at me. (And probably at David and Gillian, too.) It was insane. At one point, a Vancouver resident kept riding his bike back and forth, dinging a bell in the middle of takes. He loudly proclaimed himself a native Canadian—and then shouted at David Duchovny, "Hey, David—why did you steal my land?" I turned to the 'Chovinator and said, "He makes a salient point, buddy." I will say this about David Duchovny: he has an excellent sense of humor, and he looks great for a man who, hundreds of years ago, personally deprived the noble Musqueam people of their ancestral lands.

Being a part of *The X-Files* was one of those experiences where you just have to grab the person next to you and whisper, "Can you believe this is happening?" Then Gillian Anderson calls for security, and before you know it, your amazing experience has ended.

Where Are They Now?

Since the conclusion of the events of this chapter, these beloved characters went on to more amazing adventures . . .

- E! Entertainment Television became a twenty-four-hour source of hard-core snuff programming, until its parent company, NBCUniversal, merged with Jonny Kat–brand cat litter, and then, finally, mercifully, E! was taken off the air.
- The NBC executives who attempted, on several occasions, to cancel *Community* went on to fruitful careers spent mishandling and canceling several other things that you once loved dearly.
- Not long after the successful reboot of *The X-Files*, David Duchovny and Gillian Anderson were finally married, in a private ceremony in Maui. However, the bizarre wording of their marriage license required that their characters— Special Agents Fox Mulder and Dana Scully—be killed off, angering millions of fans worldwide.
- Joel McHale reached page 110 of his memoir and still had not even gotten to the stuff about meeting President Obama or getting addicted to oxycodone, and all the additional stories where he makes out with well-known actresses.

LIES AT TWENTY-FOUR FRAMES PER SECOND

HOW I LEARNED THAT THE SPY KIDS AREN'T ACTUAL SPIES

y the time this book is released, the *Spider-Man* franchise will have been rebooted five more times. Leading economists estimate that the *Spider-Man* reboot industry will create 175,000 new jobs: craftspeople hired to build sets, other craftspeople hired to tear down those sets minutes after they're built, plus countless performers, crew people, and visual effects artists, who, in keeping with *Spider-Man* franchise history, will be set adrift on ice floes once their work is complete. But 2004 was a much different time. Back then, getting a job on the first second *Spider-Man* movie was a huge deal. And that's what happened to a young actor named me.

This was months before I was cast on *The Soup*, which, if you've been paying attention, was a time of creative stagnation for me. And so landing the pivotal role of the bank manager in one scene of the first *Spider-Man 2*[1] was a big deal. At first, I was terrified that the Internet fanboys would crucify me because my eyes weren't the same color as those of the original Bank Manager comic book character. But the director, Sam Raimi, explained that I'd be playing a brand-new character created just for the movie, and that Bank Manager wasn't one of the classic Spidey supervillains, and that I should also stop using the bathroom in Tobey Maguire's trailer.

I was supposed to be on set, in what I had assumed would be a form-fitting, garishly colored spandex bank manager costume, at six a.m. So naturally, I was up at three a.m., and my own spider-sense was tingling ("spider-sense" is a fun name I had given my irritable bowel syndrome in early 2004). I was nervous to be shooting my first-ever movie role in the first-ever *Spider-Man 2*, so I went for a run.

I did this a lot early in my acting career, before I discovered the wonders of private gyms and sleeping pills. I would bolt awake, my mind racing with all the lines I had forgotten to memorize, and I'd burn that excess nervous energy with a predawn run through the streets of Los Angeles. I'd jog past other, equally terrified actors. "Bank manager in *Spider-Man 2*," I'd say breathlessly as we passed. "Third bikini girl in *2 Fast 2 Furious*," he or she would reply, and we'd part ways.

Spider-Man 2 was a massive, bustling movie set. On my first day, Sarah came along, because she is an incredibly supportive spouse and also because we planned to pass her off as an extra, so we'd both

---

[1] Working title: *Spider-Man Too—On the Move!*

get a free lunch. We got to meet Alfred Molina—Doctor Octopus himself—and he was incredibly nice. I think he recognized the flicker of panic in a young actor's eyes and took pity on me. So he whisked my wife away for a guided tour of the set and left me alone with my increasingly nervous thoughts, offering no acting advice other than, "Please, call me Al."

But my fears were unfounded. I did not mess up, and everybody was very kind and supportive. When I showed off my homemade bank manager costume, the entire crew chuckled appreciatively, and Sam Raimi put his arm around me to murmur, "We talked about this. Take that ridiculous thing off or you're fired. And do not—I repeat, DO NOT—change your clothes in Tobey's trailer."

Rosemary Harris, the actress who played Peter Parker's aunt May,[2] could not have been more gracious. In between camera setups, she'd recount fascinating stories about being a classically trained Shakespearean actor. She even explained iambic pentameter.

"It's quite like singing," Rosemary mused in her mellifluous British accent. "Don't think of it as the bars of a prison, boxing in your intent as an actor. Think of it rather as bars of music. You can play that music however you'd like, as long as you simply mind the notes, my boy. Now, if you'll excuse me, I need to climb into a harness and pretend to be attacked by metal octopus arms." What an amazing woman.

Spider-Man 2 opened a few weeks after the premiere of *The Soup*

---

[2] The next three Aunt Mays will be Jennifer Aniston, Gabrielle Union, and Eddie Redmayne.

and broke box-office records, and best of all, I did not get edited out of the final cut.[3] My acting career was officially figuratively *on fire*—and literally, in my own brain. In reality, that movie was the first in a string of big breaks that were great experiences but that ultimately led to nothing. Well, they all led to money. And health insurance. And residual payments. And free lunches. And sometimes free clothes. But career-wise, I found it hard to build "movie momentum," which is not a phrase anyone in the film industry actually uses. But that didn't matter, because I desperately needed some of this movie momentum.

Take, for example, the 2005 movie *Lords of Dogtown*—a film about the creation of modern skateboarding. The production would feature highly detailed re-creations of 1970s California surfing culture and thrilling skateboard stunts. I couldn't wait to hop on a board and show off my moves. Unfortunately, I was cast in the role of local news reporter Paul Moyer, a well-respected TV journalist and notoriously shitty skateboarder. I shot for an entire week on that movie, and in the final cut, they used one, admittedly pivotal, line: "Thanks for talking to us, Jay."[4]

Even after the horrible indignity of having only one line in a forgettable skateboarding movie,[5] I hung in there. I landed a role in the 2009 Steven Soderbergh movie *The Informant!*, alongside

---

[3] Although Sam Raimi stopped taking my numerous calls about not seeing any Bank Manager action figures on the shelves of local toy stores.

[4] This is a line of dialogue that people ALWAYS shout at me on the street. "Yo, *Talk Soup* guy! Say it! Say, 'Thanks for talking to us, Jay'!" I've learned to be gracious about it.

[5] It was no *Gleaming the Cube*, I'll tell you that.

Chubby Matt Damon.[6] The same day I was cast, I appeared on my friend Adam Carolla's radio show. Adam is a very skilled talker. Like, he talks *a lot*. I think he is actually paid by the syllable. As of this writing, Adam has been speaking, uninterrupted, since his first season on *Loveline* in 1995. You're a dear friend, Adam, and I cherish you. He didn't hear that, because he's talking right now.

Anyway, Adam was talking about my big break in a Steven Soderbergh movie, and then he started talking about other Soderbergh films, and he paused for a second to let me agree with him, and then Adam said that *Ocean's Thirteen*—another Steven Soderbergh movie—was crappy. This put me on the spot. I didn't want to be a Hollywood suck-up and not reply truthfully, but I also wanted to be the kind of Hollywood suck-up who still gets cast in movies with any of the various Matt Damons. Adam briefly paused, to draw in more oxygen for talking, and so I quickly agreed that, yeah, *Ocean's Thirteen* was, you know, not as good as *Ocean's Eleven*.

A week later, I reported to the set of *The Informant!* and I could tell immediately that something was wrong. Steven Soderbergh and Chubby Matt Damon were being weirdly distant. They wouldn't return my high fives, or my fist bumps, or my offers of back rubs. I soon learned that Steven had heard my appearance on *The Adam Carolla Constant Talking Show*, and he was pissed. Matt Damon, as one of the thirty-seven main characters in the *Ocean's* franchise, was personally offended by my comments.

"Oh crap," I thought to myself. "They both see *Ocean's Thirteen* as

---

[6] Which is everybody's second-favorite Matt Damon, in between *Team America* Puppet Matt Damon and Frighteningly Skinny Matt Damon.

the pinnacle of their respective careers. And my comment was, to them, an insult on par with the film's getting egregiously overlooked on Oscar night." I was freaking out. I went up to Chubby Matt Damon, trying not to stare at any of the parts of his body that he'd made chubby for his acting. "Uh, Matt, I—" He immediately started cracking up.

"I'm sorry, this was just a joke we were trying to play on you," he chuckled. I looked over and saw Steven Soderbergh smiling. Chubby Matt Damon nodded good-naturedly. "And the joke isn't working." Relieved, I cried out, "Just like *Ocean's Thirteen*!" And I went for a double high-five that they both ignored. They are both good guys with a healthy sense of humor about themselves and the business. In fact, we've got a long-running shared joke where they don't collaborate with me on anything, ever, since the release of *The Informant!*

The first time I was offered a movie role without having to audition was when I played a smug dickhead in 2011's *What's Your Number?* "They don't need you to read for this part of a wholly unlikable prick," my agent beamed. "They said you'd be perfect for the role of a vile, unredeemable wretch of a human being." I hung up the phone, elated. People were getting to know Joel McHale!

I experienced many other firsts while making that movie. It was the first time I got to touch Anna Faris's breasts.[7] Sure, this was just for a scene, so it was technically her *character's* breasts and my *character's* hands. And it wasn't direct contact, it was through a T-shirt— since Anna demanded that I wear gloves made of T-shirt material

---

[7] BUT IT WILL NOT BE THE LAST.

on both of my hands. "But it still counted as a boob touch," I breathlessly explained to my wife over dinner that night.

During the making of *What's Your Number?*,[8] I was approached about my first-ever nude scene. Which led to another first: the first time I refused to perform a nude scene. The filmmakers wanted my character to show his bare butt, and I—along with my ass cheeks—blanched at the thought. I felt that my nudity was not integral to the plot and seemed exploitative. Also, the producers refused my request of a several-thousand-dollar raise. So they opted to hire a body double—which meant I got to be a part of behind-the-scenes movie magic, by thumbing through hundreds of Polaroids of naked asses. And believe me, I was picky.

This was an important decision. For generations, members of my family would see this bare butt—as it stood in for my own, slightly more expensive butt—when they gathered together for their annual Christmas Eve ritual of watching *What's Your Number?* So I rejected all of the initial applicants in the Joel McHale Ass Rodeo[9] and asked to see a second round of firmer, plumper rear ends. I believe the word I kept using was "juicier," until someone in the studio's human resources department asked me to stop. And I realize the irony of this situation. After years of struggling to land roles in Hollywood, here I was, Mr. Big Shot, blithely dashing the dreams of hundreds of aspiring butt doubles. I had become a monster. Finally!

My experience on *What's Your Number?* was ultimately a lot of

---

[8] Actual number: 129 on the list of 2011's top-grossing movies.
[9] © Joel McHale.

fun, and Anna Faris was a wonderful costar. We bonded over a shared love for our hometown, Seattle, and on my last day of shooting, I shouted, "Go Seahawks!" and went for a double high five that she ignored. Anna is a great gal with a healthy sense of humor about herself and the business. In fact, we've got a long-running shared joke where she doesn't collaborate with me on anything, ever, since the release of *What's Your Number?*

With my next role, in *Ted*, I officially entered the "cornucopia of douchebags" phase of my career, where I showed up in big studio comedies as the smug boss, or the smug ex-boyfriend, or the smug both. Seth MacFarlane, who directed and cowrote *Ted*, encouraged improvisation. In one scene, I was supposed to insult Mark Wahlberg's character. So like the skilled improviser I am, I just kept making fun of his height. I called him a "hobbit," I compared him to "fellow little person Ryan Seacrest," and I even referred to him as "Squirt." Halfway through the scene, I had the distinct thought that Mark Wahlberg, with his average height and above-average upperbody strength, was going to kill me. But Mark was either charmed by my rakish performance or not at all threatened by me, because he just laughed it off. Seth MacFarlane called "cut," and I went for a double high five that they both ignored. They are both good guys, each with a healthy sense of humor about himself and the business. In fact, we've got a long-running shared joke where they don't collaborate with me on anything, ever, since the release of *Ted*.

I've done a lot of cool stuff in movies. I was cast in the fourth *Spy Kids* film and flown out to Robert Rodriguez's studio in Austin. I thought, "*Now* I'm gonna witness some real movie magic! No more standing in front of a stupid green screen, like I do every week on

The Soup." When I arrived on set, Robert showed me the green *and* blue screens that would be used to simulate the backdrops of the fourth *Spy Kids*. This was truly the big time!

Appearing in *Spy Kids* meant I was finally in a family-friendly movie—one that I could watch with my wife and two young sons. It also meant that I got to make out with my costar Jessica Alba, on camera, for money. It was great. My family got to see me in a real big-screen adventure—as I repeatedly leaned in to kiss Jessica Alba's warm, pillowy lips. Jessica and Robert Rodriguez are both good guys with a healthy sense of humor about themselves and the business. In fact, we've got a long-running shared joke where they don't collaborate with me on anything, ever, since the release of *Spy Kids 4*.

In the supernatural police thriller *Deliver Us from Evil*,[10] I achieved every actor's dream: playing a character who wears a backward baseball cap and is referred to as an "adrenaline junkie." The film was directed by my friend Scott Derrickson.[11] I got to have an intensely choreographed ax fight in the movie and then have a dramatic death scene. The "death" part took me by surprise during production, since as soon as I'd read the words "ax fight," I'd immediately stopped reading and begun training for my big ax fight.

There were a lot of heavy-duty stunts in the movie, which I couldn't wait to attempt. I had been injured so many times in my adolescence that I figured this was the payoff. For once, my physical antics would be preserved on celluloid, and my brother Stephen,

---

[10] Working title: *Ghost Cops.*

[11] Thanks for also casting me as the bank manager in *Doctor Strange*, buddy! Nepotism pays off.

with his stupid brittle bones, wouldn't be there to get in my way or break my fall. This time, when I regained consciousness, I wouldn't be lying on my childhood bedroom floor in my jammies—I'd be lying on a movie set floor, wearing a backward baseball cap, and super-producer Jerry Bruckheimer and super-Australian Eric Bana would be the ones asking me if I knew where I was.

But unlike in my childhood, this time I was given a stunt double. During the ax fight, my character falls down a flight of stairs. Now, these were movie stairs—which meant they were fully padded and given an hour-long meal break. I wanted to try the stunt myself, so on the first take, I flung my body down the movie stairs and ripped open a gash on my movie arm. I gritted my teeth, wanting to appear tough. "I got a boo-boo," I whimpered to the filmmakers, and they rolled their eyes, nodding to my stunt double. He then threw himself down those stairs a half dozen times. "You're really good at that," I mumbled to him as an assistant wiped away my tears and applied a single *Spy Kids* Band-Aid to my arm. During another scene, my stunt double had to ram himself into a wall—and in the process, he actually knocked himself out for a couple seconds. "Well, I can do *that*," I bragged as an assistant applied soothing balm to my macchiato-scalded lips. I later learned that my stunt double actually went to Princeton—which we all know has one of the finest stunt training programs in the Ivy League.

Throughout my movie career, I have been lucky enough to work with some of my comedy heroes. I was in a film called *The Big Year*, which was about a bird-watching competition. It didn't make a lot of money and abruptly ended the entire bird-watching-competition movie craze. But I got to meet and work with Steve Martin, who was a relaxed, kind, and thoughtful costar. Essentially, he was an inverse Chevy Chase. I have also met Martin Short, who is equally as delightful as Steve Martin. Therefore, I can give an aggregate Rotten Tomatoes score of, let's say, 77 percent to the cast of *¡Three Amigos!* as human beings.

Not long after I appeared in *The Big Year*, I performed stand-up at Carnegie Hall[12] and Steve Martin actually showed up to watch. So I'm up there, telling jokes about Tila Tequila, and I look in the crowd and there's Steve fucking Martin, looking back at me with his fucking serene, benevolent comedy-Buddha eyes. After the show, he greeted me backstage and introduced his friend, the acclaimed author Joyce Carol Oates, because that's just how Steve Martin rolls. He was incredibly gracious and casually recalled how *he* had once performed at Carnegie Hall. This was back in the seventies, when Steve Martin, you know, totally redefined stand-up comedy as an art form and sold out entire stadiums. That night, he said very nice things about my performance, asked what a Kardashian was, and then quietly left. Steve Martin is a good guy with a healthy sense of humor about himself and the business. In fact, we've got a long-running shared joke where he doesn't collaborate with me on anything, ever, since the release of that bird-watching movie.

I got to star in a movie with Robin Williams, which was a huge honor. But better than that, I got to know Robin Williams—as a human being, not just the comedic whirlwind people assume he always was. He was actually a remarkably quiet and gentle man. When Robin heard something he thought was funny, he'd grow almost

---

[12] Thank you again for bringing that up.

wistful. He'd laugh and then softly say, "Ah, fuck me." That was how he showed his appreciation. Sometimes it sounded like his Popeye voice, which made it even more endearing. Pretty soon, the entire cast of *A Merry Friggin' Christmas* (except for the kids) was saying this whenever we joked around. Robin's little conversational tic had become ours, too.

When the news broke of Robin's death, I received a text from Tim Heidecker, who costarred in the movie. The text simply read, "Fuck me."

MY STRUGGLE WITH DYSLEXIA

A HEARTBREAKING CONFESSION THAT DOUBLES AS AN EXCUSE FOR WHY I EMPLOY GHOSTWRITERS

PERSONALLY WRITED BY ACTER MAN JEOL McHLEA[1]

As a professional entertainer, I love the sound of laughter. Bringing joy to others, through my craft, motivates me almost as much as my love of money, free shoes, and making so much money that I could easily buy my own shoes, thereby increasing the perceived value of the free ones. But there is one type of laugh that I cannot stand—and that is the mocking chortle of someone who has discovered my darkest secret: that I, Joel McHale, published author, have always had difficulty reading.

It's not that I find reading to be boring, or dull, or whatever a third synonym for "boring" might be.[2] I actually suffer from a form of learning disability. In second grade, professionals evaluated me, and they told me I was a "slow starter"—which is a really positive,

---

[1] And reinterpreted, revised, and heavily edited by my ghostwriters.
[2] I even gave up halfway through reading the thesaurus entry on "boring."

encouraging thing to tell a kid who has trouble reading. I would find out, many years later, that I am actually dyslexic.

I first noticed a difficulty with reading comprehension in grade school. While the other kids were gathered around the jungle gym, sipping their juice boxes and comparing notes on the inherent Freudian symbolism of *Hop on Pop*, I myself just stared, dumbfounded by how dumb I found myself.

When I looked at words on a page, they just did not make sense. Like right now, as I gaze at this page—as it has been either shoved into my hands by my sweaty ghostwriters or put in front of me in a voice-over booth—I see a series of jumbled letters. Imagine trying to read Shakespeare while drunk, or road signs while drunk—that's the best way that I, and the Scotch I'm currently drinking, can describe this experience.

My mom took notice of my learning problem when I started getting horrible grades in English classes. My father didn't, because he is also dyslexic. "Great job on your chemistry homework," he'd say, handing back the Thai takeout menu I had just given him. And then we'd both laugh, because neither of us knew what was on the paper I'd handed him.

But my mom—who was a professional newspaper editor for the *Mercer Island Reporter*[3]—was initially tickled by my sloppy sentence structure. Then she grew concerned, then terrified, and finally looped all the way back to stunned amusement. As someone who fixed others' grammar for a living, she found my struggle with

---

[3] Sample headline: "More White People Converge upon This Tiny, Wealthy Community. Rain Tomorrow."

the English language to be noble but still hilariously askew. And as a compassionate but firm parent, she insisted that I practice my reading skills. When that failed, she threw her hands in the air and just did my homework for me.

Before you go judging my mom, remember that she was raising two other sons while juggling a full-time career alongside the world's cheapest, most accident-prone husband. Also remember that her actions led to my current career—and the lavish meals to which she and my dad are treated on a regular basis. As I sign the dinner check, I always shout, "Thanks for lying for me, Mommy!" We all get a good chuckle out of that one.

Parent-assisted dishonesty aside, I knew that if I did not take steps to remedy my dyslexia, it would grow more daunting and isolating as I got older. So I began a strict regimen of lying and cheating in order to get through elementary and middle school.

And high school. And college.

And graduate school.

I'm not proud of this. Well, not *super* proud. It is pretty cool that I made it all the way to the writing of my own memoir—for which, I should point out, I am being well compensated—before I even had to address my reading difficulties. But I do carry around a measure of shame[4] about my history of academic deceit and masquerade.

In high school, friends would allow me to copy off their tests. As a college athlete and—briefly—a fraternity member, I discovered the hidden network of stolen answer keys that has sustained both

---

[4] It's in a small vial tucked into my left sock.

of those sacred brotherhoods for generations.[5] I made it all the way through some of the highest levels of academia without being a functional reader. Sadly, it wasn't until I was hired by a basic-cable channel to tell jokes about *The Bachelorette* that my reading ability actually became a serious issue.

I wasn't illiterate—I had devised a clumsy way to stumble through things I could not avoid reading, like parking tickets and prenuptial agreements. But when forced to wade through countless jokes about *The Littlest Groom* on a teleprompter, my loose grasp of proper syntax was exposed for the crude charade it was. Just kidding—the producers just assumed that the words were scrolling too fast. But once we had fired our eighth consecutive teleprompter operator, I was forced to consider that perhaps I had some responsibility in this matter.

I worked diligently on improving my teleprompter skills. I resolved to demystify the written word—reading wasn't something ephemeral and mysterious, like welding, but something mechanical and dispassionate, like lovemaking. It worked—to the point that *The Soup*, in its last couple seasons, aired live episodes. And not once did I mangle the pronunciation of "Teresa Giudice."

These days, I'm a voracious reader, plowing through the audiobook versions of beloved classics and my favorite genre—fantasy epics where people are frequently beheaded by wizards.[6] And I'm no longer afraid to ask for help. Many times on the set of *Community*, I would shove a script under the nose of Jim Rash or Gillian

---

[5] As detailed in the 2000 release *The Skulls*.
[6] Thank you, Joe Abercrombie.

Jacobs and demand, "What's this say?" And they'd laugh, because I was pointing at my own name on the front cover. Then I'd ask them what was so funny, and they'd get sad.

Now when I tuck my two young boys into bed and they want to hear me read *Hop on Pop*,[7] I smile and say, "That's your mother's job. I'm the guy who wears makeup for a living." Then I give them each a warm hug and head down to the basement, where I drink a glass of Scotch and ear-read the latest chapter in *The Mists of Dragon-Glen: The Head-Remover Saga*.

So that's really it. My struggle with reading is the only skeleton in my closet.

Except I also drink a lot. Like, every night. Definitely way more than I should. But I have it totally under control.[8]

---

[7] Or Cormac McCarthy's *Blood Meridian*. Depends on their mood.

[8] To be continued in my next book, *Little Girl Lost: It Wasn't a Joke, It Was a Cry for Help* (as read by Jim Rash and Gillian Jacobs).

12

SUCCESS AT LAST!

FUN STORIES ABOUT MAKING OUT WITH STRANGERS

had fought, and clawed, and pretended to be able to read my way to the top of one of the Hollywood heaps.[1] Success had been a slow burn for me. Please understand that I'm not complaining— I'm merely bellyaching. The lesson I learned was to just stick around. Building a career in the entertainment industry is a lot like being hazed. In the past, I would have turned my nose up at the idea of having to "prove myself," but since making a living as an actor was way more important to me than the University of Washington rowing team, I gutted it out.

So in the beginning, when the Hollywood community said, "Hey, newbie, shave your head and eyebrows and fill this pillow," I didn't quit and say, "No. That doesn't seem right, Scott Bakula." I stuck with it—because I learned that almost everybody else will ultimately

---

[1] There's no single heap in Hollywood, but instead several different Success Piles of fairly equal height.

give up. They will decide that spending three hours a day in traffic in order to not land a walk-on part in a forgettable sitcom isn't worth it. They will move back to their hometown and try to open a microbrewery with their brother-in-law. They will be spared the fickleness of Hollywood—but they will also be spared the chance to make out with Jessica Alba, or meet the president, or talk to the president about making out with Jessica Alba.[2]

At one point, I glanced around and realized that I was appearing on television shows, and movies, and other television shows where I got asked about the television shows and movies I was appearing in. It was occasionally confusing, but other than a few awkward times at home when I thanked my wife for "having me on the show," everything was going great. I was finally practicing the craft I loved and could move on to the next step: selling out.

For as long as I have been a professional working actor, I have also been a *commercial* actor. I don't mean that I've only appeared in popular, commercially appealing projects—a quick scan of my credits will tell you that simply is not the case.[3] What I mean is that even during the brief period when I took acting seriously, I still supplemented that passion with delicious cash—which, as previously mentioned, I obtained by appearing in commercials.

And before you scoff at my obvious money boner,[4] you should keep in mind that I'm just being honest and forthright with you

---

[2] Turns out Obama is a huge *Into the Blue* fan.

[3] Six seasons and an entire Internet streaming service bankrupted!

[4] Partially concealed by these new Hanes© boxer-briefs and their Flexa-rection Boner Control™ panel.

about how it really is. All your favorite shows[5] are funded by advertising dollars, and the biggest, most sincere Hollywood stars will still appear in commercials—it's just that *they* do voice-over work, so as to conceal their cash blushes and money boners. It's the Hollywood acting community's dirty little secret.[6]

I've always appeared in commercials, and I always will—as long as my looks, popularity, and product-gripping fingers maintain their respective elasticity. I've done so many ads that my representatives—the agents and publicists who get a chunk of my income—actually became alarmed. After one particularly fruitful[7] year, my commercial agent turned to me and nervously explained that he couldn't secure me any more work within the advertising world. Seconds later, I had lifted him off the ground by his neck.

"I meant for the rest of the year!" he wheezed as my insatiable bloodlust and moneywant forced my hand to clench his windpipe ever tighter. "You can still . . . do more . . . *next yeeeaarrrr!*" I released him. Once he regained consciousness, my agent explained that large corporations have rules for the celebrities who advertise on their behalf. Essentially, if you appear in one company's commercial, you can't turn around and then do one for their competition for a certain period of time. So if I appeared in a Dr Pepper ad, I couldn't then skip across town and drop my drawers for Mr. Pibb for at least a year, no matter how much I wanted to. So here was my agent informing me, with great disbelief, that, due to my aggressive pursuit

---

[5] Except for those on cable or streaming services *(see footnote 3)*.
[6] Other than how many of us have accidentally run over drifters. I know what you did last summer, Dame Helen Mirren.
[7] And shameless!

of high-paying advertising work, there was no other part of my soul he could auction off.

I had appeared in commercials for the Ford Fusion and made ads for a dissolvable energy tablet (manufactured by a giant pharmaceutical company that once—and this is true—marketed heroin for cough suppression). I had hawked ice-cream bars, vodka, doughnuts, and a fitness tracker to keep tabs on all the ice cream, vodka, and doughnuts you're ingesting—plus digital cameras, cell phones, credit cards, razors, and video games. I had advertised for every kind of thing that human beings buy and consume to distract themselves, aside from pornography.[8]

Here's the thing: I sincerely love acting, bringing life to unique characters, and knowing that people might be entertained by my work. But I also enjoy making money, and providing for my family, and providing for my other, secret family in Idaho.[9] I firmly straddle the line between art and commerce—and I look great while doing it.[10]

Once I became a recognizable, somewhat beloved personality, I was ushered into the realm of celebrity—where I was warmly greeted by other recognizable, somewhat beloved personalities. My wife and I would get invited to these well-attended Hollywood events, and at first, we would nervously walk the perimeter of

---

[8] And only because your offer came in too low, PornTube.

[9] I love you, Beth, Riley, and Crispus!

[10] Thanks to these Hanes© boxer-briefs and their Straddle-Firm™ anti-bunching technology.

the party, not sure how to strike up conversation with all the famous Jennifers and Matts and Mariskas.

But thanks to my acting work and incessant televised advertisements, I eventually burst through a membrane[11] and found myself able to casually chat with legendary performers. Michael Keaton once walked right up to me and started talking, like we were old friends. I still get nervous when a former Batman approaches me, but I have found some conversational touchstones that make it less awkward.[12] At some point, Sarah and I went to a party and she marveled about how we personally knew all the famous people in attendance: "Isn't it kind of weird that *we* know all these people?" We had done it—we were now real Hollywood assholes! Upon this realization, Sarah and I held each other lovingly, and then we spotted a young couple at the party who were too green and nervous to approach anyone else, and we laughed and laughed. Michael Keaton, Val Kilmer, George Clooney, Christian Bale, Ben Affleck, and Adam West all thought it was funny too.[13]

A s a handsome actor, I have kissed several former costars. And while the idea of pretending to be intimate with a stranger, in front of a camera crew with their weirdly bulging cargo shorts

---

[11] Not a metaphor—there's a thin, viscous diaphragm at the entrance to every big Hollywood party.

[12] Sports, getting in shape for roles, how heavy Batarangs are, etc.

[13] The next three Batmans will be Chloë Grace Moretz, Bow Wow, and Eddie Redmayne.

pockets, may sound awkward to you, I can assure you that it is incredibly sexy, and profitable.

For the most part, kissing a costar is just one more surreal experience for an actor, among many—like when your body gets scanned for an action figure mold, or when you have to pretend that a tennis ball is a larger, computer-generated tennis ball that will be added in post-production. Frankly, some of the greatest acting of my career is at the end of a long shoot day, when I return home to shrug my way through an explanation of what I did all day on set—when what I did all day was kiss a handsome, comely, shapely actress.

But I have a very earnest way of talking with my wife about this. I say, "Sarah, sometimes, when an actor and an actress pretend to love each other very much, they kiss. And that's where babies come from." She is usually so delighted by my intimate knowledge of human sexuality that she asks for no further details.

Sarah knows that I love her, and she's very pragmatic about some of the weird, sexy stuff I have to do as an actor. Basically, she knows what side the bread is buttered on. And she also knows what I do to pay for that bread, and therefore doesn't need to hear the actual details of the buttering. And so, I will share those details with you instead, because I have been told it will goose book sales.

I hope you understand: I am not a creep. I simply took detailed notes on all the costars I have kissed—sometimes before the kissing was even completed. You could say that . . .

THEIR KISSES IS ON MY LISTS!

A LIST OF THE PEOPLE I HAVE BEEN PAID TO MAKE OUT WITH

KISSEE: Brie (Alison)

NARRATIVE JUSTIFICATION FOR KISSING: Our characters Annie and Jeff had a real "Will they or won't they?" relationship. As in, "Will viewers be nauseated when they remember that Annie was eighteen when the show began and Jeff is clearly in his forties? Or won't they?"

LIPS: Creamy, soft, spreadable—just like Brie (cheese).

DURATION OF KISS: 8 minutes, aggregate, through six seasons and no movie.

KISSEE: Gillian Jacobs

NARRATIVE JUSTIFICATION FOR KISSING: Our characters Britta and Jeff had a real "Will they or won't they?" relationship. As in, "Will viewers care about this portrayal of actual human connection, or will they just want another paintball episode, or won't they?"

LIPS: Hard, cold, and unforgiving (I missed her head completely and accidentally kissed a concrete divider).

DURATION OF KISS: 43 minutes, aggregate, through six seasons. This means that Gillian and I are technically married in South Carolina, Nebraska, and Maine.

KISSEE: Lauren Stamile, aka hot professor lady from *Community*

NARRATIVE JUSTIFICATION FOR KISSING: My character was briefly paired with a more "age-appropriate" partner because viewers were "getting grossed out" by the Jeff/Annie thing.

LIPS: Mature and commanding. Reminded me of my own impending mortality, and therefore, she had to go.

DURATION OF KISS: 2 minutes, 14 seconds, aggregate.

KISSEE: Katharine McPhee, *American Idol* runner-up and *Community* guest star

NARRATIVE JUSTIFICATION FOR KISSING: Our characters were supposed to make out a lot during an entire episode. So we made out a lot during the production of an entire episode.

LIPS: Tender, inviting, with spot-on pitch control—although not as nice as the lips of your 2006 American Idol, Taylor Hicks!

DURATION OF KISS: 3 minutes, aggregate.

KISSEE: *Gilmore Girls* star Lauren Graham, who told me I could just call her "Lauren," but whom I feel duty-bound to refer to only as "*Gilmore Girls* star Lauren Graham"

NARRATIVE JUSTIFICATION FOR KISSING: Our characters in *A Merry Friggin' Christmas* were very friggin' married, so we kissed a couple times.

LIPS: Tremulous, well moisturized, released direct to home video.

DURATION OF KISS: Approximately 3 smooches and 1 peck.

KISSEE(S): Mila Kunis-Kutcher and a totally nude female body-builder, from a deleted scene in *Ted*

NARRATIVE JUSTIFICATION FOR KISSING: My character—a smug jerk and sexual deviant—wanted to lure Mila Kunis's character (I think she was named "Kila Munis") into a smug threesome with a totally nude female bodybuilder, to more effectively reveal the sexual deviant aspect of his personality.

LIPS: Cute, approachable, with a surprisingly durable bond with former costars (Mila); taut, strong, and with a pierced labia (NOT Mila).

DURATION OF KISS: N/A (Scene was not included in the final cut of *Ted*, and therefore didn't need to have taken place, be filmed, or released as DVD bonus content. Even though it was.)

KISSEE: Meryl Streep

NARRATIVE JUSTIFICATION FOR KISSING: None. Meryl kissed me on the mouth, perhaps accidentally, after I introduced her at a gala sponsored by a fashion magazine.

LIPS: Naturalistic, lived-in, with a flawless Hungarian accent.

DURATION OF KISS: A couple of seconds, for which she received her twentieth Oscar nomination.

And now, some members of the KKK (Kissing Klose Kalls!)

A SHORTER LIST OF PEOPLE I NEARLY MADE OUT WITH

DREW BARRYMORE—played opposite my smug ex-husband character in 2014's *Blended*. Although we did not share a kiss, I did make the attempt—both on camera and later, near the craft services tent.

ELIZABETH BANKS—I recorded a character voice for the children's video game *Lego Dimensions*. I didn't make out with anyone, but during the production, I accidentally swallowed a Wyld-style Lego. That character is voiced by Elizabeth Banks, and it took me a couple days to pass the plastic figure, therefore this counts.

 KATEY SAGAL—played opposite me on *Sons of Anarchy*. There was no kissing, but she was topless in the scene, and her real-life husband was in the room. So I get points for that.

 JIMMY SMITS—played opposite me on *Sons of Anarchy*. There was no kissing, but his character did beat me up, which gave me an erection. So I get points for that.

13

SUCCESS, AT LEAST

A SOBER REFLECTION ON ALL I HAVE SACRIFICED
IN ORDER TO PLAY MAKE-BELIEVE FOR A LIVING

t seems to me, as one of my ghostwriters desperately thumbs through a dog-eared copy of *Literary Metaphors for First-Time Memoir Coauthors*, that fame is a free toothbrush you are handed at the end of a dental checkup. After much scraping and suctioning, you freely accept it. But then you take it home, and it turns out to be not quite as big as you'd like, it looks weird in your bathroom, and sometimes it has someone else's name on it.[1]

As much as I extol the virtues of regular, high-profile employment in the entertainment industry, there are serious drawbacks. I will now explore these drawbacks, and if you're not listening to the audiobook, you should adjust the voice in your head—the one you imagine hearing when you read books[2]—so that it sounds very

---

[1] Jeffrey Zernghast, DDS.
[2] It's Rosie Perez, isn't it?

serious. Because this next part of the book is no-bullcrap, real-deal life stuff, you guys. It's important. So important that each problem fame and success have brought me is typeset in CAPITAL LETTERS, <u>UNDERLINED</u>, and **BOLDFACED** so that you can more effectively imagine **THE VOICE OF ROSIE PEREZ SCREAMING THESE WORDS AT YOU.**

I don't want to seem unappreciative or spoiled. I'm sure, as you read about my amazing life, lucrative career, and amusing stories from the set of *Lords of Dogtown*, you're saying, "This guy shouldn't complain. I'd give anything to have just a fraction of his fame, money, and skateboard movie anecdotes!"

But look—it's not easy being me. Sure, it's frequently, almost consistently great—but I didn't achieve all of this by settling for "great." No, I achieved it through hard work and perseverance.[3] Sure—no person can have everything. And that's the most difficult aspect of success: "everything" is the one thing that you don't have yet. When you're rich and famous, you look at other people's designer backpacks and samurai-sword iPhone cases, and you think, "I want that." It's a very human, positive philosophy—and one that will ultimately lead me to absolute fulfillment. Just as soon as I have everything, which includes fulfillment.

Here are the challenges that face me. And this list is ever growing, so check back for updates.[4]

MY FAMILY DOESN'T GET TO SEE ME AS MUCH AS

---

[3] And luck, genetics, networking, and the public's desire to hear jokes about *Dancing with the Stars*.

[4] My publisher is saying I can't have a hardcover book that self-updates. Evidently, the technology doesn't exist. Again: Why can't I have *everything*?

THEY WOULD LIKE. Myself and my lady-wife, Sarah, have brought two flaxen-haired boys into this world, Eddie and Isaac. And my hugely successful career does not provide my sons with enough time to let me enjoy the simple pleasures of watching them grow, teaching them how to use bladed weapons, and supervising as someone else brushes their flaxen locks with the ivory combs each was gifted on his third birthday. I love my sons and want nothing more than to be able to spend more time with them. But they seem preoccupied, with elementary school, and Legos, and finding dates for their senior prom.[5] I guess they just can't make time for their "old man"—a nickname I have forbidden them from using, because it could hurt my chances as a viable romantic lead.

My family and I can't always get our schedules to sync up. I hate to drag our private squabbles into the public eye, but I just don't understand why it's such a big deal for them to find some time for me. I long to share every fun and enriching adventure in my career. Just once, I'd like to roust the kids out of bed at four a.m. for a quick flight to the River Cree Resort & Casino in Alberta—where they can watch me perform stand-up comedy for two thousand adoring drunks—without my wife complaining about their missing out on schoolwork or important vaccinations.

I love my sons, and I wish I could watch them watch me enjoy the fruits of my labor. But I'm so busy, I don't even know what fruits or labors they're allergic to.

And because I am taken away from my family so often, my wife

---

[5] I am so busy, I am not certain of my sons' ages. But I'm fairly certain that they're both somewhere between four and nineteen.

doesn't always have the time to hear about what's going on with me. I want to share all these amazing things with her—what kind of cheese plate the casino left out for me or the funny sound effects that "Buckwyld and the Shizz" played on my morning radio appearance—but she's distracted by the frivolous details of our home life, usually saying, "The boys just set the dining room table on fire. I gotta go."

I wish I could be the husband and the father they seem to want.[6] For now, I am but a ghost—a wraith who passes through the halls of our home, on his way to an appearance on *Late Night with Seth Meyers*. "I was here, my loves . . . ," I will whisper to them. But they will not be able to hear, because I am already gone. And also because the limo driver has really cranked the A/C, and the granola bar I'm chewing is awfully crunchy. "Sir, is something wrong?" the driver will ask as I wipe away a tear. "This vent was pointed right in my face," I will reply as I take another bite.

NO ONE WILL LET ME INTO THEIR HOLLYWOOD CLIQUE. If you're rich and famous, you don't want to hang out with the "normals."[7] You want to kick back with people who understand the bizarre nature of your job, who will bask alongside you in mutual career envy, and who will cast you in their ensemble comedies. Therefore, you need to be a part of one of the industry's many "packs"—cliques of like-minded celebrities who have banded together throughout Hollywood history.

In the sixties, it was the legendary "Rat Pack"—a group of suave entertainers who joined forces upon realizing that they all resem-

---

[6] Or "need." Yeesh—clingy much?
[7] Or the "sobers."

bled humanoid rodents. Then there was the "Brat Pack," the "Frat Pack," and the "Christine Lahti Pack"—each one comprising the most popular performers of their respective eras.

I'm ashamed to admit that I've always desperately wanted to hang out with a group of cool, accomplished, and creative peers. I mentioned this recently while hanging out with Nathan Fillion, Dax Shepard, and Jimmy Kimmel. I think they understood. They all grew quiet once I brought it up and then left my house shortly thereafter.

I'd love to get in with Judd Apatow's crew, but he keeps using the old Hollywood excuse of "not liking me personally or professionally." I came this close[8] to joining Adam Sandler's clique when I appeared in the movie *Blended*. Sandler's group includes sports commentator Dan Patrick, NBA legend Shaquille O'Neal, and former UN secretary-general Boutros Boutros-Ghali[9]—but I guess there was no room at the inn for little old me. I also costarred in Seth MacFarlane's *Ted*, which I figured would cement my membership in the "Mac Pack" . . . but no. All it got me was a role in one of the most popular comedies of all time. Swing and a miss again, McHale!

This eats at me so much that I even turned to Nathan Fillion, Dax Shepard, and Jimmy Kimmel to ask if *they* knew of anyone cool or successful enough to hang out with me—and they said no, and that they all had to get off the phone for various reasons.

I could start my *own* Hollywood "pack,"[10] but honestly, that seems

---

[8] I'm holding my thumb and forefinger three millimeters apart right now.
[9] He was that "You can dooo it!" guy.
[10] I'll call it "the Hollywood Ten"!

like a lot of thankless work. First, you have to get an Evite account, so you can send out invitations to your secret clique parties. And then you have to special-order personalized satin jackets for everyone—and then return Christian Bale's over and over again, until you get his size right.[11] Worst of all, you have to fend off all the desperate celebrities who want to be a part of your new clique. It's more trouble than it's worth. So if anyone is reading this, and you need a tall, sarcastic, handsome guy[12] to fill out the roster of your Hollywood clique, please send all requests to my publicists.

I DON'T ALWAYS GET RECOGNIZED EVERYWHERE. What is one of the worst parts of fame? Ask any celebrity and they'll tell you: not getting approached in public. There is no worse feeling for a professional movie or TV actor than walking through an airport terminal, or eating your lunch, or using a public restroom, without being stopped by a stranger for a five-minute conversation about where they recognize you from. When you are allowed to pass through your day like a normal person, it is a cruel reminder that for a celebrity, the work never stops. Every time someone doesn't nudge me at a urinal, or chooses not to take up-skirt[13] shots of me on a hotel room balcony, or doesn't ask me to record a voice mail for their girlfriend, it troubles me deeply. This means that either they want to give me some personal space and privacy, or worse, my fame is ebbing. So, please, remember: When you see a celebrity in public, do not hesitate to remind them that they are famous, and that you are acknowledging their fame. Interrupt their dinner, tug forcefully at their

---

[11] "It's for a role!" he keeps saying. Whatever, fatty.
[12] Who just happens to make a killer bean dip!
[13] What I wear on vacation is *my* business.

sleeve, or just shout the first thing that comes to mind. The least you can do is insist on multiple photographs, preferably taken by someone who doesn't know how to operate your cell phone camera.[14]

I know the pain of not always being recognized, and it leaves me with an empty, gnawing sense of want—one that I'll have plenty of time to ponder the next time someone asks me to pose for a selfie with them.

THERE ARE STILL SOME THINGS I DO NOT RECEIVE FOR FREE. Our society rewards the rich and the famous with free designer clothes, cars, beds, and car-shaped beds. The act of showering the wealthy with items they could easily purchase brings a comforting balance to the universe. But it doesn't go far enough.

Sure, my closets are brimming with free shoes, ill-fitting jackets, laptop computers, gaming systems, sporting goods, and cutlery. Whenever I enter a celebrity-attended event—like the opening of a shoe, computer, or cutlery store—I am just handed bags of this stuff. I have grown so accustomed to this that when I actually *do* have to pay for something—like water, electricity, or shelter—it's like being rudely awoken from a dream.[15] Sure, I got a free car . . . but no one told me I had to pay for the gas to make it go! And I was handed a two-thousand-dollar leather jacket, but I had to pay to have it dry-cleaned![16]

It's a tease. And if I spent more time with my children, one of the

---

[14] If your phone isn't even powered on, and then the camera's flash settings are disabled, this means you *really* care.

[15] One of those dreams where you show up naked to school because no one gave you free clothes.

[16] And then pay shipping on its replacement after I learned it was never meant to be laundered.

first lessons I would impart[17] is that it isn't nice to tease people. Certainly not rich and famous people, because they are the unfortunate few whom life has not prepared for mockery.

If society is going to provide celebrities with free things, then society needs to quit dicking around and go all the way. Not letting us get absolutely everything in life at no charge is the economic equivalent of blue balls.[18] And the fact that I, as a well-compensated professional actor, have to pay for my own elective surgeries is a disgrace—not just to me, but to this country and the entire calf implant industry.

Please remember that entertainers sacrifice much to bring you joy. And all we ask in return is wealth, and popularity, and total privacy, and attention, and lavish praise, and free stuff.

---

[17] After my first lesson: who I am and what I'm doing in their house.

[18] Technically, green-blue balls. Not to be confused with blue-green balls, which—if you have them—should be examined immediately by a medical professional.

MY SON NEARLY VOMITED ON OUR NATION'S FIRST AFRICAN AMERICAN PRESIDENT

BARACK OBAMA'S BRUSH WITH GREATNESS

Once you have reached a certain level of fame and success, you will be asked to host high-profile events. I recited this sentence in the mirror, over and over again, every morning for six years. I did this because of a self-actualization technique I learned about in one of those books that Oprah makes you buy. I just can't tell you which one, because it's a—wink!—*Secret*.[1] Anyway, the technique worked, and soon I was offered several hosting "gigs."[2]

I was asked to host the Independent Spirit Awards, where I stood in front of Hollywood's elite and referred to the Mila Kunis/ Natalie Portman drama *Black Swan* as "that movie where the girl

---

[1] Also, I can't remember the name of the actual book. Again, I have reading comprehension issues.

[2] Or as jazz musicians refer to them, "jobs that help you buy heroin."

from *That '70s Show* eats out Luke Skywalker's mom." My parents were there, and I remember looking out into the audience and seeing their faces, reddened with pride. The cunnilingus joke I had disguised as a celebration of independent cinema then led directly to more hosting opportunities: the Writers Guild Awards, the ESPYs, and most notably, the 2014 Cox Communications Executive Management Forum.

I was also asked to host an exclusive event in Aspen where CEOs, high-ranking military officials, and Hugh Jackman all gathered to discuss issues that were relevant to them—like the economic impact of global climate change and how difficult it is to get gravy stains out of adamantium claws. And I'm not exaggerating about the guest list; this was a super-secret, high-security, moderately well-catered event that brought together heavy hitters like John McCain, the head of the NSA, and Non-Chubby Matt Damon.[3] It was intimidating and nerve-racking to tell jokes in a room full of those who had protected the nation, entertained millions, and been monitoring my phone calls and emails since the second Bush administration.

I was in awe of these people and their various mutant powers, so I decided to be honest and straightforward. I began by saying, "I'm not gonna lie—not even under oath, as many of you have—this is an intimidating event. Sure, you all put your pants on one leg at a time, just like everyone else. But when *you* put your pants on, an oil company payoff falls out of the pockets." They all laughed, because the joke was absolutely true, and because their human-behavior simula-

---

[3] He had just finished working on *Behind the Candelabra*, and simulating fellatio on Michael Douglas burns a lot of calories.

tion chips instructed them to do so. I was literally speaking truth to power, and power was smiling back and saying, "Now, isn't that cute?"

The interesting thing about really powerful people is that they generally have a good sense of humor about themselves, since they know, deep down, that they can send you and your loved ones to a work camp. I casually insulted these titans of industry—right to their ruddy, jowly faces—and they seemed to love it. I joked about how they all would meet up later to hunt poor people, I accused George Lucas of selling Ewok meat on the black market—it was great. So great that it led to an offer for something even bigger: a hosting job for the Costume Designers Guild Awards! . . . And after that, I was invited to tell jokes in front of the president of the United States[4] at the 2014 White House Correspondents' Dinner.

This is an annual event that brings together politicians, celebrities, athletes, journalists, the president, the First Lady, and Baba Booey. A comedian is invited to close out the dinner, and this gig has served as a career milestone for many comic performers. My invitation to host meant that I'd be filling the impressive podium elbow dents of Stephen Colbert, Conan O'Brien, Jimmy Kimmel, and, most memorably, the Peiro Brothers.[5]

I was going to be performing stand-up comedy in front of the leader of the free world, Hollywood's best and brightest, the Washington elite, and Baba Booey. I was thrilled. And then they told me how much I was going to be paid: ten thousand dollars. I thought

---

[4] (of America!)
[5] They were jugglers.

that was a joke at first, which is why I laughed for several minutes on a phone call with the White House Correspondents' Association, the organization that hosts the dinner.

"Mr. McHale, this is a historic event. It is considered a great honor just to be invited. Baba Booey will be there," they insisted over my peals of laughter. In order to sweeten the pot, and to get me to stop giggling, they threw in a couple nights at the Washington Hilton,[6] and I begrudgingly agreed to accept this solemn honor.

As the nice lady on the phone, and my agents, and my wife kept reminding me, this was a big event with an impressive list of attendees. All of which put me in the awkward position of having to make an actual effort, and also made me feel something that I had not experienced in years, if ever: *fear*. I did *not* want to screw this up, no matter how lousy the pay was—so I committed myself to actually trying.

I immersed myself in current events and political news, so that my monologue would be informed, urbane, and feature lots of jokes about New Jersey governor Chris Christie's weight. For each of the previous events I'd hosted, my material had to be vetted in advance by publicists, lawyers, and Zooey Deschanel's high school friend—to ensure that I wouldn't tell jokes that could be deemed offensive by costume designers or Zooey Deschanel.

But the White House Correspondents' Dinner was different. Since it is hosted by a private organization and broadcast on the nonprofit, nonviewed channel C-SPAN, I would have no such limi-

---

[6] The site of past Correspondents' Dinners, the 1981 attempt on President Reagan's life, and the 2017 Gathering of the Juggalos.

tations. I could say whatever I wanted, and there was nothing that anyone—not even Zooey Deschanel—could do about it.

I reached out for advice, hopping on the phone with past Correspondents' Dinner hosts whose assistants had not been instructed to block my calls. Jimmy Kimmel, Conan O'Brien, and Craig Ferguson all provided helpful insight; no such luck with the Peiro Brothers, who were evidently too "big-time" and "deceased" to answer some simple questions. Seth Meyers gave me a valuable piece of advice, which was echoed by every previous host I spoke with: "Since nobody needs to see your jokes beforehand, protect them."

"Like walnuts!" I exclaimed.

Seth continued, "If somebody asks to see your material, politely say no." He explained that, as host, the responsibility for the jokes was mine alone; no one else needed to see them, and if they *did* read them, the organizers would only get nervous, or leak my sophisticated Chris Christie fat jokes to those jackals in the press.[7]

So, leading up to the big night, I collected jokes—hoarding them, polishing them, and refining them.[8] Keeping my material under wraps was challenging, because in the months leading up to hosting the White House Correspondents' Dinner, the only thing people asked about was what kind of jokes I was going to tell.[9]

I got to Washington, DC, a few days before the event, and I was focused on turning in a polished performance. So I trained—like I was a long-distance runner, or a guy who was going to tell some

---

[7] The same nice, cheap jackals who were paying me ten thousand dollars.

[8] Like walnuts!

[9] Followed immediately by, "Are you nervous? You must be really nervous!"—which is super helpful.

jokes in front of Michelle Obama and the *Duck Dynasty* guys. I had a tiny binder with all my tiny jokes inside. That thing was glued to my hand for three days,[10] and I practiced with all the commitment of a lifelong C-student who has a reading disability. But the pressure was starting to mount. All those people asking if I was nervous, and insisting I should be nervous, and then explaining if I bombed, my career would take a huge hit, must have somehow gotten to me.

The pressure came to a head the night before the big event, when I hosted a dinner for my family and friends. They had joined me in Washington for the honor of watching me perform, and the bigger honor of potentially meeting the *Duck Dynasty* guys. I looked around at my loved ones and Kyle MacLachlan,[11] and the full, overwhelming scope of the Correspondents' Dinner, and how much expensive wine my family had just ordered, began to hit me.

This was truly absurd: I, Joel McHale, would soon be entertaining the president—and, in my excitement, I had agreed to pay for travel and accommodations for nearly a dozen other people.[12] Every moment of my career had somehow led me here. Every failed audition, every near-accidental almost-suicide, every joke about *The Celebrity Apprentice*—they had all built to this moment, where I had to cover a couple-thousand-dollar dinner tab.

The emotions welled within me as I raised a glass to toast my guests: "Tomorrow night will be a big milestone in my career and in

---

[10] Thanks to an incident at a DC-area OfficeMax.

[11] He'd followed me home from another dinner years earlier, and my parents had said I could keep him.

[12] I even bought tuxedos for two of my writers—which I forced them to wear every day when they ghostwrote this book.

my life. So I want to thank you for being here, for letting me buy you dinner, airfare, two nights at the Washington Hilton, and in some cases formalwear. Here's to you, and your uncanny ability to spend all my money."[13] The room fell silent. Everyone seemed very touched by the sentiment.

The big day had finally arrived. No longer would people be able to ask me, "Are you nervous?" Instead, they would have to ask, "Are you nervous *for tonight?*"

My guests put on the tuxedos I had purchased for them, and we were on our way—to potentially witness the end of my career.

Before the Correspondents' Dinner, the attendees—who will soon be crammed into a hotel ballroom—are gathered, so that they may be crammed into a smaller room, for a meet-and-greet with the president and First Lady.[14] At this point, I was an hour away from the biggest performance of my life. And this is when things started to get even more surreal, because celebrities and powerful media tycoons and all their various mistresses and boy toys were lining up to have their photo taken with the president. I looked around and saw Robert De Niro, Sofia Vergara, Mindy Kaling, Fred Armisen, Lupita Nyong'o—it was like a big Hollywood production.[15]

My family, as is their custom, had clustered near the bar. They were chatting as I obsessively ran through jokes in my head. Sarah doted on our youngest son, Isaac, who was not feeling well. He'd

---

[13] My best guess—and this is not an exaggeration—is that I spent just over $30,000 total on that trip. And that includes Kyle MacLachlan's second order of chicken fingers.

[14] Following the requisite search-and-squeeze from the Secret Service.

[15] All it was missing was two young Caucasians to serve as the lead characters.

looked a bit clammy that morning, so we did what any caring, concerned parents would do—we shoved him into a tiny tuxedo and
dragged him to meet the leader of the free world. It was really important for me and Sarah that the boys get a photo with the president and First Lady. We wanted them to have a record of this
cherished memory, before they eventually sued us for emancipation
in their early teens.

Everyone was waiting for the president and First Lady to enter
the room. The excitement was palpable—as palpable as the vomit
Isaac promptly spewed onto the carpet near my feet. As waiters and
a surprisingly helpful Fred Armisen all lent a hand, my mother-in-
law, Sally, tapped me on the shoulder. "Somebody stole my purse,"
she informed me.

"We are *literally* in the most secure room in the universe right
now," I replied.

"Ask that shifty-looking man if he saw anything," she insisted,
pointing across the room.

"That's the president," I muttered.

"Oh, here's my purse. It was behind this little vomiting boy," Sally
mused.

We quickly tidied up, hosed off Isaac with the bartender's soda
gun, and were ready to meet the Obamas.

The president and the First Lady were remarkably cool. I guess
when you've sent a team of SEALs to shoot Osama bin Laden in the
eye socket, it's not too big of a deal to meet the *Soup* guy. Nevertheless, they were polite and seemed alarmingly normal—particularly
for a Kenyan-born Muslim and a woman obsessed with outlawing
all sugar.

I had been wondering what President Obama and I would talk about. He was, arguably, the most powerful person on Earth,[16] so what heady topics would we discuss? Chinese trade restrictions, the destabilization of the Greek economy, the deadlock in Congress? My family was called up, we greeted the Obamas, and the president promptly turned to me and said, "So, they bringing *Community* back for another season, or what?"

The experience of meeting the president was like a ride at Disneyland.[17] You wait in a long line, the most exciting part lasts just a few seconds, and then you're spit out into an empty hallway, breathless and dazed. Later, someone shows you a photo to prove that it happened.

The McHales meet the Obamas at the 2014 White House
Correspondents' Dinner. My son, Isaac, a longtime Republican,
is hiding his face in protest.

---

[16] Other contenders: Beyoncé and the guy who plays the Mountain on *Game of Thrones.*

[17] But oddly, nothing like the Hall of Presidents.

The Correspondents' Dinner is an entertainment and comedy event designed by well-intentioned people who do not understand either of those things. It is also governed by odd traditions. Rather than being introduced and entering from offstage, the featured comedian sits on the dais—for over an hour—right next to the First Lady. So all those people who asked you, for months, if you were nervous can now look right at you and say, "Boy, he looks nervous." Michelle Obama was very down-to-earth. We talked about our kids, and healthy eating, and how many dumbbell curls she can do. But in the back of my mind, I kept obsessing over my jokes.

President Obama spoke before me. Yes, this event is so bizarre and lopsided that the president of the United States warms up the crowd *for you*. In this case, Obama killed.[18]

He had great jokes and expert comedic timing, and I just sat there, in awe, thinking, "Shit. This dude just destroyed the room.[19] How do I follow that?"

I was introduced, and I got to my feet. For a couple seconds, I actually thought I might pass out. But then, something kicked in—and it wasn't the dose of elephant Xanax I had considered taking. Serenity washed over me as I stepped to the lectern. I looked out at that odd gathering of Americans, and I thought to myself, "I am either very well prepared, or I have just died and am ascending to heaven. And gosh—Diane Lane and Wolf Blitzer sure make a lovely couple."

---

[18] Six insurgents with a drone strike during the dinner. Also, he was very funny.
[19] And an Afghani wedding party with a misguided drone strike.

That is definitely a strange room in which to tell jokes. The front tables are the most powerful people in the world; the middle tables feature celebrities, other notables, and Baba Booey; and the back is nothing but drunk, raucous, underpaid journalists. So the laughs usually start in the back of the room and rush forward, as they trigger the human-behavior simulation chips in our nation's elected representatives and their mistresses and boy toys.

I'm proud of the job I did that night—I feel like I was evenhanded, doling out insults to the overweight *and* the politically bankrupt in equal measure. I wrapped up my performance and was so relieved it was done that I nearly kissed the president. But I had a feeling he wouldn't reciprocate, mostly because I had just finished telling a five-minute string of jokes about him killing people with drone strikes.

The Correspondents' Dinner after-parties are surreal and absurd—and I don't just mean the mini hamburgers on pretzel buns. Hours after my performance, I found myself at the Italian consulate, alongside Jessica Simpson, a member of the Russian protest group Pussy Riot, and Hank from *Breaking Bad*. "Now, *this* would make one wacky reality show!" I shouted at the three of them. Hank from *Breaking Bad* just asked me why I'd made them all stand together near the salad station.

The next morning, the nerves and excitement of this historic experience finally left me—along with all the mini hamburgers I'd eaten with Pussy Riot. You see, dear readers, Sarah and I had both caught Isaac's stomach bug. So, on our flight back to Los Angeles, we celebrated a job well done by taking turns befouling an airplane bathroom. In forty-eight hours, I went from telling jokes in front of the president of the United States to mewling in agony atop a tiny toilet, with my cargo pants bunched around my ankles.

God bless America!

"Good job, Joel. I loved your joke about how I used a robot-plane to blow up a hospital. Great stuff."

JOEL McHALE'S SPONSORED MEMORIES

Fond Remembrances of Days Past, Presented Here as Unique Marketing Opportunities for Products and Companies

PRESENTED BY

AND

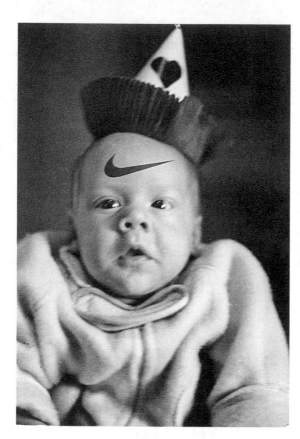

A young clown is born.

The neonatal dermatologist asked my parents if they'd like my birthmark removed, and they replied, "Just Do It."

Relaxing with my brothers down at the ol' gravel pile, soaking up the rays and enjoying a refreshing Mountain Dew® Kickstart™ Midnight Grape.

The happy family in Italy. L to R: My mom, Laurie, holding my youngest brother, Stephen; my oldest brother, Chris; my dad, Jack; me; and the Swiffer® Steamboost™ powered by Bissell®.

A day of firsts: my first time telling jokes in front of a green screen, and my first glimpse of the stylish lines and expert handling of the 2017 Porsche Macan GTS.

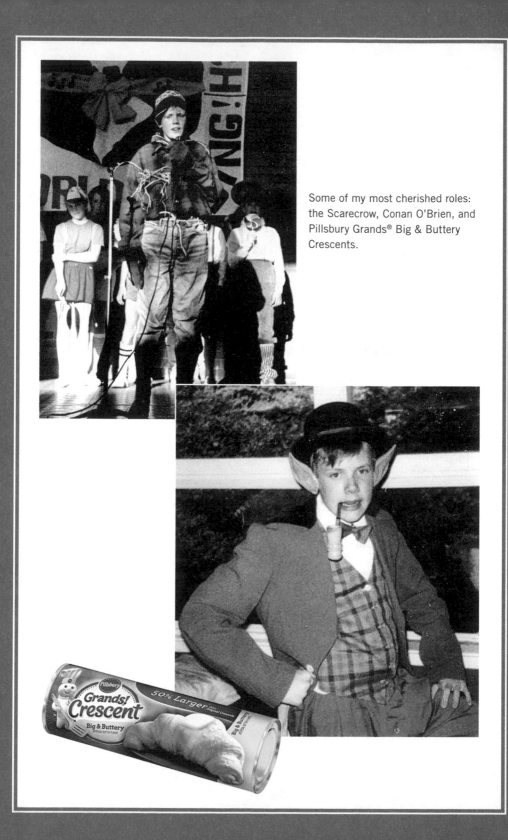

Some of my most cherished roles: the Scarecrow, Conan O'Brien, and Pillsbury Grands® Big & Buttery Crescents.

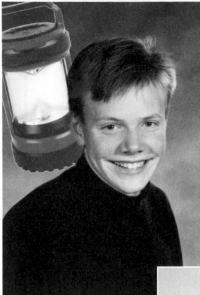

Middle school, and my future was looking bright—almost as bright as the Coleman® Conquer™ Spin™ 550L Rechargeable LED camping lantern.

Sarah and me, young and in love—like two peas in a pod. Or even better, like two peas in Birds Eye® Steamfresh® Chef's Favorites Lightly Seasoned Garlic Baby Peas & Mushrooms.

On a family vacation with Sarah, Eddie, and Isaac. A wonderful day that could never be wiped from my memory, except perhaps by the cleaning power of Chore Boy® Ultimate Scrubbers.

CROSS-JOEL

Test your reading retention skills, and the very limits of your sanity, with this mildly challenging crossword puzzle that's all about Joel!

Have fun!*

Across

3. Joel put this in his mouth once
5. Sexual position which likely produced Joel's brother Stephen
6. Joel's blood type, probably
8. Joel's XBox Live gamertag
12. Not the name of either of Joel's sons
14. Anagram for synonym of "puzzle"
17. Defunct pizza chain whose existence Joel had to be convinced of
20. Celebrity who will be most upset by the publication of this book
22. Shooting location of "X-Files" reboot
24. Seven random vowels and one consonant
26. Shoe brand pivotal to Joel's success
27. They compiled this puzzle
29. "Police Academy" star, if his name had one less "T" and he invented movable type for printing presses
30. The best classic movie monster, objectively speaking
31. Joel's loudest brother
32. Common crossword answer
34. Proper response when someone asks, "You were born in Rome?"
35. Subtitle of Joel's "Spy Kids" film
36. Joel appeared on this Seattle sketch comedy show

Down

1. Second word in title of ninth chapter
2. U.W. football team that Joel kind of played for
4. Mammal that Joel fears the most
7. Another way to spell the first name of Joel's "Community" character
9. Person who has not appeared in book yet
10. Reggae artist best known for "Here Comes the Hotstepper"
11. The sound of an agitated dog who gets interrupted
13. Not the name of Joel's wife – but not NOT the name of Joel's wife
15. Pacific Northwest city where Joel did not grow up
16. They tried to destroy "Community"
18. Joel's beloved catchphrase
19. Joel put this in his mouth once
21. Childhood trauma which explains much about Joel
23. One of Joel's favorite oyster varieties
25. "Double Jeopardy" star Judd, or Joel's childhood cat with rancid breath
28. Site of many of Joel's stand-up comedy appearances
29. Also not the name of either of Joel's sons

* Answer key available to readers who provide photographic proof of their purchase of four or more copies of this book.

PICK A DICK!

Put your knowledge of Joel's diverse filmography to the test, and **draw lines** connecting the **roles** of this Man of a Thousand Faces with the corresponding **names** of his various smarmy, arrogant characters!

"Wilbur"

"Mark"

"Jeff"

"Warren"

"Rex"

"Hudson"

"Boyd"

WROD JEMBUL:
An Empathetic Word Search

Locate the names of companies and products for which Joel has served as a compensated endorser. But remember: Joel suffers from dyslexia, and therefore all the answers are scrambled within the puzzle.

```
W  B  F  O  P  U  K  I  R  O  D  Y  V  A  T  F  U  T  W  O  V  L
A  V  R  B  G  P  M  R  D  P  I  R  U  M  S  E  M  M  E  Q  L  O
L  Y  G  G  X  G  T  I  I  C  L  A  A  G  E  T  Y  B  C  H  E  G
B  O  S  B  E  Q  Y  O  M  W  Y  M  F  K  X  X  C  P  K  K  G  M
A  P  G  U  P  U  A  F  V  K  X  F  B  E  I  X  X  Q  L  O  E  F
L  F  F  O  N  X  R  E  O  T  V  Z  H  K  C  S  V  N  O  E  L  O
X  V  P  F  E  K  B  K  C  K  G  E  S  A  A  T  R  I  N  Y  T  H
K  V  T  E  F  M  I  C  N  V  Z  Q  B  G  N  J  Z  W  D  R  I  M
E  C  Q  C  R  R  I  N  M  I  X  W  U  S  P  W  K  U  I  H  T  Q
N  G  J  I  H  P  O  N  D  J  G  D  G  S  R  T  S  N  K  C  I  B
L  Y  D  Q  O  D  F  S  I  U  R  J  M  R  E  Y  B  J  E  O  C  O
O  Y  O  M  K  G  B  A  U  S  N  K  O  U  S  T  I  U  B  S  Z  R
C  B  F  V  J  V  Y  H  C  D  E  D  O  U  A  H  T  Y  A  V  D  A
O  L  U  X  L  X  X  O  O  T  I  N  O  J  M  P  F  F  R  B  D  C
F  H  M  I  R  H  H  U  H  B  K  N  D  T  E  H  I  U  D  X  R  C
W  N  P  N  C  A  A  W  H  I  O  P  O  S  R  S  T  A  I  S  J  E
O  N  O  N  T  E  N  D  I  S  X  L  J  O  L  O  B  M  I  T  E  I
Q  F  E  I  R  N  A  D  C  E  I  G  L  I  R  L  R  P  H  U  M  P
```

CLUES:

- Car model that replaced the Taurus (in the marketplace, if not in our hearts)

- Brick-based video game featuring branded characters

- Purveyors of circular breakfast pastries

- Combination cooler/chargrill device of dubious safety

- Cellphone carrier that got rid of the hot motorcycle girl

- Frozen confection that has led many to engage in desperate dares

- Men's razor conglomerate and owner of cheating NFL team

- Hard-to-find wheat-based clear spirit

- "I once got busy in a _____ _____ bathroom!"

- Creators of the Power Glove

- Dissolvable energy wafer from former heroin producer

- Minuscule activity tracker/guilt-causer

- Credit company that still won't give Joel a "black card"

SCRAPE 'n SMELL!

These scratch-points have been infused with a **wide variety of scents** that are intimately associated with Joel's career!

Scratch the areas below and **inhale the greatness.***

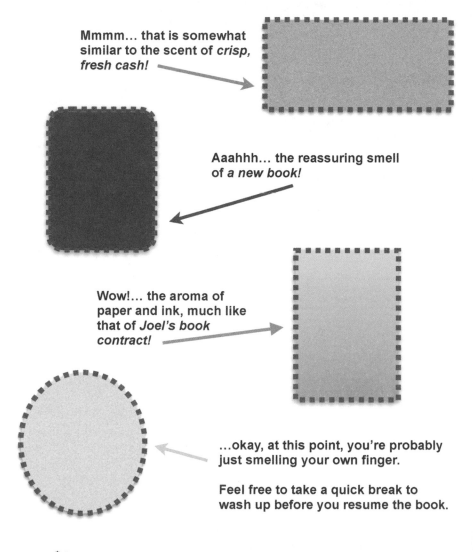

Mmmm... that is somewhat similar to the scent of *crisp, fresh cash!*

Aaahhh... the reassuring smell of *a new book!*

Wow!... the aroma of paper and ink, much like that of *Joel's book contract!*

...okay, at this point, you're probably just smelling your own finger.

Feel free to take a quick break to wash up before you resume the book.

* Due to technological limitations, e-books are unfortunately exempt from this feature. So just sit there and wait quietly until the physical book owners are done. Thank you.

PART II

BE A BETTER YOU BY BEING MORE LIKE *ME*

HERE'S THE SELF-HELP PART OF THE BOOK

CELEBRITY DIET SECRETS REVEALED![1]

LOSE WEIGHT AND LOOK FIT, SIMPLY BY STARVING YOURSELF AND EXERCISING CONSTANTLY

f I am to guide you on the path to a greater life, a fitter body, and a plumper, more muscular wallet, then I need your absolute, un-wavering trust.

Take off all your clothes, right now.

If you're reading this on an airplane, find a discreet corner to fully disrobe—maybe between the beverage carts. Or if you're reading this in an actual bookstore, just go ahead and get naked, since you're likely the only person there. Go ahead. I'll wait.

All right, now—present yourself fully nude, in front of this book, so I can get a better look at you. Okay. Turn to the left. Lift that one

---

[1] First secret: Use exclamation points whenever possible. Shouting burns a lot of CALORIES!!!

thing there . . . all right. Pull that . . . whole area . . . apart. Great, I've seen enough.

Before I give you my professional opinion as a working actor, I want to ask, "How do *you* feel about your body?"

- 74 percent of you will have just answered, "Not good. I'm a mess."
- 19 percent of you will have just answered, "I look okay, but I have some work to do."
- The remaining 7 percent will have replied, "I look and feel great. But I could always feel even *better*, I suppose."

First, the good news: Each of those answers is correct. Now the bad news: You all look terrible. Before you slam this book shut in anger, please understand that the truth can be difficult to hear— and that I want to help you improve yourself. Also, remember that you are still nude, and slamming a book shut in this state puts you at a much greater risk for paper cuts.

I will help you control your eating habits, develop a workout regimen that actually works, and reshape your physical form. I care deeply about your self-esteem and your feelings.

So don't close the book.[2] Instead, *open your mind*. And also, keep reading, because that's how books work, dummy.

---

[2] Or eat it, chubbo.

. . .

Y ou *can* transform yourself—I speak from experience. When I
started on *The Soup*, my body was encased in suits the entire
time, so I really let myself go. I had no self-control. When I required
sustenance, I would eat—sometimes even foods that I enjoyed. And
when exercising, I would occasionally stop if I felt I was causing injury to my joints and muscles. I was paying attention to my body
and its limitations. I was happy, carefree—and as a result, I was a
stupid, sloppy, disgusting mess.

Then I was cast on *Community*. This was a *real* acting job—one
where I was fully objectified and treated like a piece of meat. It was
exciting and then daunting. During the first season, my character
was required to disrobe for a narratively crucial scene of strip bil-
liards.[3] I was going to be naked, bent over a pool table in a room
full of strangers, and for once, it would actually be filmed. When I
thought of the dozens of viewers who would eventually see this as
part of NBC's Thursday-night lineup, I panicked.

I only had a few weeks before my nude scene would be shot. As
an actor, my body had never been subjected to this much scrutiny. I
suddenly felt jealous of my female costars—they were lucky enough
to experience this kind of pressure all the time and therefore were
well accustomed to it. But I didn't have time to dwell on gender pol-
itics and how unfair they were to me. I had a lot of work to do.

---

[3] Because he was a lawyer who had to return to a community college to finish his
degree.

Anyway, the day of my big scene arrived. I stripped down and looked like this:

So how did I do it? Through my patented three-step process—which I call "the Joel McHale Patented Three-Step Process."[4]

Legal Disclaimer: Before we dive in, my lawyers have asked me to reiterate that I am *not* a medical professional.[5] Therefore, any advice I offer about diet or exercise should be taken with a grain of salt (and only *one* grain of salt, since that's what I recommend eating as a fun "cheat day" snack). These weight-loss guidelines have not been vetted by actual doctors, or actual vets. The only proof I have of their effectiveness are my rock-hard abs, my concrete-like shoulders, and my pebbly obliques. My publisher and I cannot be held responsible for how amazing you will look if you do everything

---

[4] Patent pending.

[5] Apparently not even when I wear a lab coat and stethoscope I stole from a wax-museum diorama of *Chicago Hope.*

I am about to recommend. There—that should hold up in a court of law.[6]

For my money,[7] talking to a doctor will only slow you down. After all, physicians don't have to appear shirtless on camera, so what do they know? All a doctor will tell you is, "Eat well, blah blah blah . . . exercise, blah blah blah . . . your current method of weight loss is causing severe liver damage, blah blah blah." Useless!

A doctor will only discourage you by stubbornly insisting that there is no fast, easy method to lose weight—when all they have to back up that claim is "factual evidence." Well, I don't need facts, because I have *results*! The medical community wants you to stay fat and happy, so they can rake in all that sweet triple-bypass cash. It's a scam! So listen to me, and before you know it, the pounds will be melting and screaming their way off your confused, sweaty body.

Now, I realize that any diet and exercise regimen can seem challenging at the outset. I'm not a fanatic, so I know that the first step toward a better body is a positive attitude. Possess that positivity, embrace it, seize it, and then toss it from the nearest open window. Thinking about your mental state, rather than fixating on your body, is a shortcut to fitness failure. A positive attitude is just New Age code for "pre-quitting." The human brain is nothing more than a couple of pounds of meat, which better serves as ballast weight for calisthenics exercises. So point that brainmeat toward my Patented Three-Step Process![8]

---

[6] Especially if it's that re-creation of the *Night Court* set that I saw at the wax museum.

[7] Thanks again for that.

[8] Patent declined, due to incorrect return address on patent form.

Step 1: The Threat of Public Humiliation—Nature's Little Motivator!

Any gym rat worth his testicle-shrinking supplements will proclaim, "You can't soar like an eagle if you train like a turkey." And you won't be motivated to truly push the limits of what your body can achieve, and how weird your shoulder veins can look, unless you have an awesome, truly frightening goal ahead of you. This first step is completely mental and therefore the easiest. So—get yourself cast in a high-profile acting project, and convince the writers and producers to arrange for a scene where you will appear topless.[9] Once faced with the reality of your naked form being preserved in 4K Ultra HD video for all of human history, you will have no choice but to plunge forth into . . .

Step 2: Food—It's Not for Eating Anymore!

Nutritionists and other quacks like to blather on about foods that contain "empty calories," but the dirty little secret they won't tell you is that *all* food contains empty calories. Remember that any meal—no matter how "healthy" and "necessary"—should be considered a form of weak-willed surrender committed by a bloated, simpering coward.

---

[9] If you're a woman, this scene will have been written for you in advance. Once again, the ladies have it easy!

Your body is like a spoiled brat on a road trip, constantly whining from the backseat.[10]

Don't let your body boss you around! C'mon—who's the parent around here, anyway? And whose car is this in the first place?[11] Your body will do anything to have its greedy needs fulfilled. So when it throws a tantrum—in the form of hunger pangs, dizziness, or loose teeth—do not give in. You're on the road to a fitter you.

Next stop: Skinny Jeans Town![12]

This second step is not easy—I will not sugarcoat it. I won't even stevia-coat it, since sweetened coatings of any kind are strictly forbidden by the Joel McHale Patented Three-Step Process.[13] But if you can power through the crippling migraines, the jaundiced skin, and the gnawing sensation that something is deeply wrong with your internal organs, a kind stranger will eventually approach you and say those three magical words: "You look sick." This is their jealous way of saying, "You look *great*." Your hard work is paying off!

What can you eat on this diet? The short answer is "nothing," but I learned the hard way that this isn't actually true. Or humanly possible. So I have determined the *five essential ingredients* for the ultimate fat-burning diet . . .

---

[10] *Wahhh*, I need to use the restroom and also I need sustenance to survive, *wahhh!*

[11] And what does the car symbolize? Even I'm not sure.

[12] Just as soon as we make it through Shrunken Heart Junction.

[13] Patent resubmitted via parcel post. Should arrive in two to three weeks, at which point status will be updated once more to "pending."

THE JOEL McHALE NUTRITIONAL PENTAGRAM

Five Points to Summon the Unholy Body of Your Dreams

If you want to *look* like a star, you need to *follow* a star—and only eat the things the star is pointing at!

1.

2.

5.

3.

4.

1. Hard-boiled egg—Breakfast is the most important meal of the day to not eat. Power through those hunger pangs and reward yourself at dusk with a single hard-boiled egg, consumed while standing over a sink. For a healthy crunch, leave the shell intact!

2. A nut—Sometimes you feel like one, and sometimes you are *permitted to eat* one! My diet plan has "wiggle room," so treat yourself to a single nut, of any variety, every twenty-four hours.

3. Hot sauce—Whether it's from a packet, from a bottle cap, or just slurped from your open palm, hot sauce can add some much-needed spice to all the other food items you are not permitted to consume!

4. Salmon jerky—Does it taste good? Of course not—it's a dried fish carcass. But on my plan, one strip of dehydrated salmon flesh contains 95 percent of your daily caloric intake, so you better eat some. Plus, the jerky's natural odor will keep pesky interventionists—and their desperate offers of sustenance—away from you.

5. Liquids—It is vitally important to consume fluids while on this diet. But water will only lead to unnecessary bloating. Instead, end your workouts with a bracing nutritional liquid—like red wine or an eighteen-year single-malt Scotch. Their natural pain-numbing qualities can also help silence your throbbing muscles. Combine both with your daily nut for a power smoothie!

So now you know what to occasionally put into your body. But when it's not resting or lazily begging for food, your physical form needs something to do. Which is why you should fling it, with wild abandon, into my final step . . .

Step 3: Don't Stop Quitting on Never Not Un–Giving Up to Non-Surrendering—a Simple Exercise Philosophy for Everyone

We've already established that your body is a desperate liar, shiftily grasping for any excuse to avoid bettering itself and looking great on camera. And what do we do to liars? That's right—we punish them, preferably with fearsome metal machines composed of weights and pulleys. If your neighborhood lacks a sex dungeon, then I suggest joining a fitness center—the equipment, atmosphere, and payment plan are virtually identical.

Exercise is like jury duty for your body—the only surefire way to get excused from performing it is by pretending you're a racist. And fat racists are the *worst* kind—so you better start exercising, all the time. Throughout my acting career, I've had personal trainers, gym memberships, body doubles, and—best of all—a job that gives me plenty of time to pursue athletic exercise. So try to replicate that in *your* life—or honestly, I don't know how you're gonna do it.

I got into peak shirt-removal shape for *Community* by doing constant push-ups. I would wake up and immediately start doing push-ups. I'd have my sons stand on my back while wearing diving weights as I did push-ups. I'd do push-ups until I passed out. And then, after the paramedics resuscitated me, I would roll over and immediately do more push-ups. Remember: You're not working out hard enough until your loved ones are standing in the doorway of the bathroom you're doing push-ups in, tearfully begging you to stop.

So it's really that simple—just exercise beyond the point of absolute physical exhaustion! "But, Joel, you're wealthy and therefore have access to high-tech gym equipment and adequate floor space for constant push-ups. I'm just a slob with a tiny apartment, and when *I* go out in the alley to exercise, the neighborhood kids pelt me with garbage."

I hear this excuse all the time, so it's led me to devise . . .

JOEL McHALE'S EVERYDAY EXERCISES FOR PEOPLE FREQUENTLY PELTED BY GARBAGE

- **VOLUNTEER PALLBEARER:** Every time I'm at a funeral, I can't stop thinking about all the isometric exercises I could be doing instead. But one time, while hoisting the casket of a loved one whose name escapes me, I realized something: pallbearing is a great form of exercise! When God closes a door, he opens a window—and when God takes away someone you care about, he gives you a high-intensity workout. My pro-tip: circuit train by funeral-hopping at the local cemetery and helping lower bodies into their final resting places. It can be tricky to convince the mourners to let you perform multiple reps, but that's where being a celebrity *really* comes in handy!

"Now, this is what I call a *dead* lift!"

- **WOOD CHOPPING:** You see it in movies all the time: the athletic, handsome, stoic hero who chops away at a massive pile of wood. Another character spies him through the brush and then watches as the man peels off his plaid shirt to reveal bulging biceps, rippling abdominals, and nipples like battleship rivets. Just think, that could be you: the person watching the woodsman! Crouching and shifting your weight to avoid detection is a great way to build core strength.

"I feel the burn (of illicit longing)!"

- **ALLOW YOURSELF TO BE HUNTED FOR SPORT:** Good enough for the plots of *Hard Target* and *Surviving the Game*, good enough for *you*! Find a group of wealthy, morally flexible businessmen,[14] and convince them to take you along on their next hunting excursion. Once you awake from the powerful sedative they snuck into your drink, you will be forced to run for your life as they hunt you down. Ask anyone who has been on either side of the hunting-humans-for-sport equation, and they'll tell you: you'll never feel more alive—or get a better cardio

"Your pain, my gain!"[15]

---

[14] Seacrest knows some guys. I can put you in touch.
[15] Also acceptable: "Knife to meat you!"

workout—than by reverting to your base, animalistic instincts. People will wonder how you got such amazingly defined lats, and also that cool scar on your cheek. Unfortunately, the evil businessmen's nondisclosure agreement will prohibit you from revealing the details of your workout—so just wink and say, "My new training regimen is *murder*."

So that's it! Do all that stuff and you will look just like me the next time you're shirtless on a cult sitcom.

Always remember: Don't forget to get motivated!

TURN THAT SCOWL UPSIDE-DOWL

USE SARCASM, BACKHANDED COMPLIMENTS, AND DIRECT INSULTS TO WIN PEOPLE OVER

T o better amplify your career trajectory and remorphalize your success matrices, you need to pony up, throw down, and really start crushing it with your interpersonal skills.[1] My health and fitness techniques may leave you looking like an Adonis,[2] but you can't receive your doctoral degree in awesomeness from Better U[3] unless your personality is equally charming and fearsome.

As cataloged in exhaustive detail elsewhere in this book, I have achieved great wealth, moderate influence, and the grudging, angry respect of my peers. And I owe it all to sarcasm, which is juuuust *great*.[4] Sarcasm is the universal leveler—and I've found that the best way to get a sense of equality is to place myself well above others. As

---

[1] And your jargon usage.
[2] Or his wife, Mrs. Kleinman-Adonis!
[3] A nonaccredited university.
[4] This statement is not intended as sarcasm.

a TV host, stand-up comedian, and compensated product endorser, I have traveled all over the globe, bringing my signature blend of well-aged and moderately topical Kardashian jokes to delighted crowds from Dallas, to Fort Worth, and everywhere in between. During my career, the one thing I've learned is that people absolutely love to be teased and mocked.

Yes, audiences everywhere have been ribbed . . . for *my* pleasure.

Applying the overly simplistic lessons from a successful entertainment career to real-world interactions isn't something to be done lightly. It's something to be done *often*. So once you've established your own career as a highly paid comedian and host of a satirical pop culture clip show, these guidelines for well-placed mockery will help you in any situation.[5]

Everyone enjoys a good, honest joke—particularly one directed toward them by someone who is more attractive and wealthy. This interplay helps balance the scales of an oft-unjust world. It is primal, instinctive, and beautiful. The noble manatee—one of our closest relatives in the animal kingdom—has an intricate social order built completely around sarcastic jabs and bitchy comments about outboard-motor-injury scars.

You need only hang out at an elementary school playground[6] to witness this behavior in the human world. As adults, it is easy to forget the fun and carefree days of our youth, when we'd gather for a spirited round of Look at Tony's Dumb Velcro Sneakers, and Tony

---

[5] Not yet tested in "suicide by cop" scenarios.

[6] Wear a trench coat and dark glasses so as not to arouse suspicion.

Needs the Teacher to Fight His Battles for Him, followed by Let's Find Tony's New School and Make Fun of His Dumb Shoes There. These harmless games were a vital part of growing up and left no lasting injury for anyone involved.[7]

I know full well that it is not right to single out children for ridicule. The teachers and parents at my sons' schools have pointed that out to me on several occasions. So please understand I am not advocating bullying. I am merely advocating having a little fun at the expense of others. And where's the harm in that?

So why *do* people like being mocked? Simple. Because in this endlessly distracting world of smartphones, social media, and videos of skateboarding bulldogs, a sharp, well-timed insult resonates as a reaffirmation of basic humanity. It gives the deliverer a chance to display attentiveness toward another person, through a cursory evaluation and critique of their more obvious flaws. And it allows the recipient to feel—however briefly—that they truly matter, and that their clothing choices and body type are worthy of someone else's hastily formed commentary. If I'm taking the time to cast aspersions on some element of your personality, or wardrobe, or haircut, it means I'm paying attention to you. It's my way of acknowledging the foibles of *all* people, by specifically pointing out only yours. "Hey, I'm a human being, just like you," I appear to be saying, even when what I'm actually saying is, "Your shirt is dumb."

---

[7] As far as I know. I lost touch with a lot of the old gang after Tony's bell-tower "incident."

I know these comments are valued, because many times, the person on the receiving end expresses their appreciation. "Gee, thanks a lot," they'll grumble. And I take that grumbling to heart, even though it is unnecessary. Their looks of stunned gratitude as they peer at me through tear-rimmed eyes are thanks enough.

Now you know why sarcastic comments are important to society, why they are always welcome, and how they can be spun into gold.[8] So how can you do it? Thankfully, employing your rapier wit to win admiration and bruise egos is remarkably easy, even for someone like you.[9]

It doesn't take a lot of hard work to assert yourself via sarcasm. Remember, the easiest method is always the best method. As a celebrity, you will meet and socialize with other people or other celebrities. This is the perfect setting in which to gain a foothold in the social strata and establish your delightful dominance over others. But you must act quickly. If the conversation turns too pleasant, you may be forced to accept your new acquaintances as people and be expected to relate to them. Instead, use your sharp, well-timed sarcastic observations to let everyone know who's the boss.[10]

How do I empty my quiver of sarcastic arrows into the plump, unprotected hearts of friendly strangers? I just go with the flow(chart)!

---

[8] I didn't technically explain this last part, but you'll figure it out, I'm sure.
[9] See? Also, your shirt is dumb.
[10] Technically, it's Judith Light.

JOEL McHALE'S SIMPLE "HOW TO INSULT PEOPLE" HOW-TO CHART

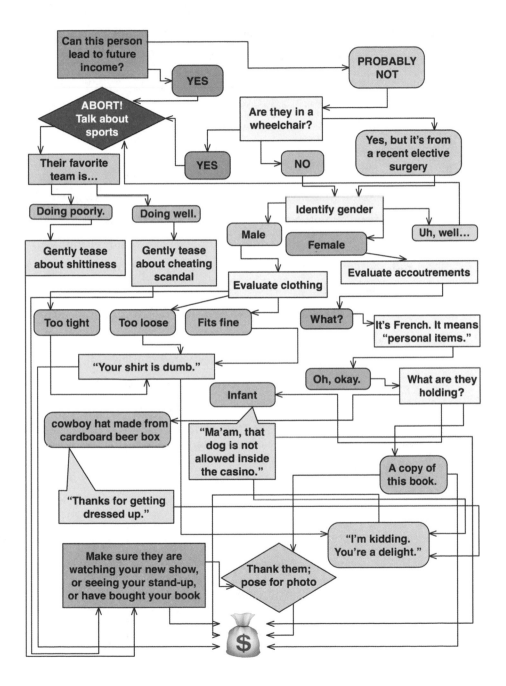

Once you have established yourself as the kind of sharp-tongued gadfly who tells it like is[11] and doesn't suffer fools, you will find that you have insulted your way into employment opportunities. In most cases, you will be hired to host a pop-culture-skewering comedy series or asked to offer your opinions on one of those "talking heads" panel shows.[12] In those scenarios, you need a cut to wider swath—so your sarcasm must be wielded as one would a flamethrower, a scythe, or a multibarreled T-shirt cannon.

As host of *The Soup*, I had to form quick opinions on a wide variety of television shows and outsized personalities. I needed a way to mock these people[13] without having to learn much about them—so I mastered the art of making blanket statements, blind assumptions, and, most challenging of all, the art of knitting blanket statements while blindfolded.

People use the phrase "shooting fish in a barrel" like that's a bad thing. But they're missing the point of shooting fish in a barrel: it's easy, it saves time, and no one gets hurt—other than the fish, and most of the barrel. Plus, shooting barrel fish alleviates the burden on our already overfished oceans and waterways. It *really* is the right thing to do, which is why I did it for twelve years on basic cable.

But be wary. Because once you have mastered this form of widespread mockery on television, people will offer you payment to perform it in person. And although that means more money, it

---

[11] Here's how it is: your shirt is dumb. Got you again!

[12] Such as Spike TV's *Byrning Down the House with David Byrne*.

[13] And by proxy, their viewers. And my viewers. And myself, I guess.

also means you must travel to other places, which puts you—once again—in the potentially dangerous position of almost relating to people.

Throughout my career as a successful touring stand-up comedian,[14] I perfected the art of winning over a crowd through casual, personalized insults. And there is nothing a paying casino audience loves more than when I poke fun at the place where they live. Yes, the art of hometown mockery is alive and well. In fact, in many parts of the American Midwest, this is the only remaining viable industry.

Here is how you do it. Once you (and your first-class travel) have been booked for an appearance on the road, do some research. But be careful—don't learn too much.[15] These people were kind enough to welcome you to their local venue and then pay you handsomely for it—the least you can do is learn three things about their city, so you can more accurately disparage it.

So while you're being shuttled between the airport and your hotel, perform a cursory Internet search. Don't dig too deep. All you need are some surface details—like the closing of a beloved local pizza place or how they recently elected a dog as mayor—and you're off to the races![16] People love it when charming outsiders stroll into town and tell them stuff they already know about the place where they currently live. It makes them feel good about

---

[14] Which was remarkably easy to launch once I was famous. Note to struggling comics: become famous *first*!

[15] Please refer back to my "avoiding empathy" lesson.

[16] During your search, do not get distracted by ads for the local horse-racing venue.

whatever life decisions may have kept them in Toledo. This is sure-fire comedy gold and guaranteed to win over a crowd.[17]

Flinging barbs at an entire city is easy! Almost as easy as getting a tetanus infection while visiting Albany.[18]

Here, I'll show you. Philadelphians, feel free to sound out the larger words—we'll wait.

Just pick one of these Hometown Mockery TenderZones™ and you'll have a killer opening line that will have those Bostonians laughing so hard, they'll choke on their bland, disappointing chowders.

LOCAL SPORTS—BECAUSE THERE *IS* AN "I" IN "INSULT"!

Athletic teams are a classic Achilles' heel for most cities. Learn one unfortunate stat about a local sports hero—like "number of fumbles" or "number of fingers blown off in fireworks-holding accident." Mention this early, and the audience will be groaning and drunkenly bellowing its way into the palm of your hand.

---

[17] Provided they are already won over by your fame and attractiveness.
[18] This would kill in Albany.

LOCAL CUISINE—YOU WON'T BELIEVE WHAT THEY DO WITH CHILI AROUND HERE!

If sentient Troll doll Guy Fieri has taught us anything, it is this: as long as civic pride is involved, people will convince themselves that fistfuls of molten cheese are actually "regional menu items." So ask the bellhop at your hotel about the most inordinately popular local dish. You will know you are on the right track if diners are awarded a free T-shirt in exchange for ingesting it. Drop a reference to this barely digestible foodwad, and the crowd will bay with approval: "He knows us, and he also knows the cherished slop that will eventually claim many of our lives!"

LOCAL NEWS—THIS JUST IN: YOUR CITY IS GARBAGE!

Has anything in the area recently caught on fire that normally shouldn't catch on fire? Point it out.[19] The applause you receive may be slightly muted, but that'll only be because many of the audience members' hands are still bandaged from battling the blaze.

---

[19] Unless it was a hospital or school.

Remember, it's never "too soon" to give a paying crowd the opportunity to shout, "Too soon!"

F ollow these guidelines and you'll always impress an audience with intimate knowledge of their small, inconsequential lives. Here—I'll demonstrate how it's done. All I need is the suggestion of a city . . . any city. Okay—I heard "Tampa."[20]

"Good evening, **Tampa!** I can't believe that **Buccaneers wide receiver** shot up the **Mons Venus Strip Club** last week. You know, **the one over on Dale Mabry Highway**. [*Pause for raucous acknowledgment of Dale Mabry Highway*] Luckily no one was injured, since bullets can't puncture the first three layers of pork in a **Cuban sandwich**."

Not only will this venue-specific material net you some solid laughs, but the goodwill it engenders can help you conceal the fact that you haven't updated your Tila Tequila jokes since whenever she was last relevant or newsworthy.

So that's it. You now possess all the necessary knowledge to insult your way to fame, fortune, and greatly improved interpersonal relationships. I'm sure you're gonna do juuuust *great*.[21]

---

[20] As have countless medical examiners when inquiring about the scene of a crime.
[21] This statement *was* intended as sarcasm. Also, your shirt is dumb.

EAT A DICK, ANGELA LANSBURY

SELECTING THE CELEBRITY FEUD
THAT'S RIGHT FOR YOU

Along your journey to successfulness and stardom-dom, one of the biggest pitfalls you will encounter is your own complacency.[1] Once you've starved and punished your body and then isolated yourself from most of your peers, it can be tempting to sit back and bask in all the happiness and contentment that this lifestyle grants.

But remember: You are in the entertainment business, and the people want a show! And every show features compelling characters and conflict.[2] It is your solemn responsibility, as a budding entertainer/actor/comedian/podcaster, to relentlessly and publicly create scenarios that will lead to friction—or as the French refer to it, *frisson*.[3] So one of the top items on your "I Want to Be Rich and Famous To-Do List" should be this: find a worthy rival.

---

[1] As well as your own prescription drug use.
[2] With the exception of HBO's *Entourage*.
[3] A light, cream-based sauce usually served at post-conflict reconciliation dinners.

Throughout history, valiant warriors have clashed with fearsome adversaries on the field of battle. Each had their mettle tested, and sometimes their testes mettled, by these conflicts. The ancient Spartans had Xerxes, the Nazis had Indiana Jones,[4] and Michelangelo had Shredder and his fearsome Foot Clan. Matching wits and wills with a high-profile foe will sharpen your competitive edge, hone your abilities, and, most crucially, lead you to invent conflicts solely for the benefit of notoriety. This is known colloquially as "engaging in a public feud."

"But I was hoping to use my wealth and fame to spread positivity and inclusiveness," you might be mewling. And that instinct, while admirable, will lead you straight to Failure City, population: not you.[5] Take a look around and you will see plenty of other people preoccupied with the well-being of their fellow humans. The betterment of society should be left to those who truly care about the future of our species: banks, insurance companies, and professional sports team owners. You can trust these entities to safeguard us, because they have "skin in the game." But as a celebrity, the only skin you should be concerned with is the skin covering the asses you put into seats. And as you embark upon this next step, I want you to stay focused on the task at hand—and keep the image of that ass skin in your mind, too.

Selecting a professional rival with whom to engage in a bitter game of one-upmanship will be a fun and rewarding aspect of your future entertainment career. And I speak from experience—I have

---

[4] And to a lesser extent, the Allied forces.

[5] Because you won't even be able to afford the rent in Failure City, you saintly loser.

seen a million celebrity faces, and I've mocked them all. Most of these targets accepted my ridicule with mealy-mouthed comebacks that weren't even worthy of my attention (usually along the lines of, "*Who* said *what*? Oh. [*shrugs*] Okay.").

In the initial phase of my career, I was taking shots at other celebrities on a weekly basis. Like an inexperienced gunslinger, I was firing randomly, occasionally hitting the mark—but just as often causing a ricochet to strike an innocent townsperson, like that kindly schoolmarm who had begged me to give up on my life of crime so she could make an honest man out of me.[6] I made a lot of noise, but at that stage, only the overly sensitive would even bother to engage me.

There was the time I incurred the brief, slurring wrath of tough-guy actor Mickey Rourke. Mickey Rourke is a fascinating person. He started out as a handsome character actor, then drifted into relative obscurity, only to resurface with acclaimed performances and a face that looked like somebody was making a bust of Marlon Brando out of cookie dough when the potter's wheel got jostled. Like any successful celebrity, Mickey Rourke was often spotted at big events alongside the requisite arm candy—which, in his case, was a half dozen tiny, trembling dogs. Rourke attributed his comeback to these magical animals, thanked them in award acceptance speeches, and described them as "the love of [his] life." Somehow, after making these public proclamations, he avoided criminal investigation.

I stand before you now somewhat chastened by what happened next. You see, I have since become a proud dog owner, after welcom-

---

[6] It's okay—she made a full recovery from that gunshot wound and lived to the ripe old age of twenty-nine, when she died of tuberculosis.

ing an adorable, urinating animal into our family.[7] So I now understand what a devoted pet can mean to a person—especially if that person has to appear in direct-to-DVD Bulgarian action films. But at the time of Mickey Rourke's seventh professional comeback, I was just a young, hungry punk scrappin' for a fight. So I made a joke on *The Soup* about the passing of Rourke's beloved Chihuahua Loki—the dog, I assume, who helped Mickey learn his lines during production of *The Wrestler*. He took this slight in classic Mickey Rourke stride—by which I mean he publicly threatened me with violence. At least, I think he threatened me. Even after poring over the footage, it was hard to tell, due to the many peculiar acting choices Mickey Rourke has made in his portrayal of Mickey Rourke.

Approached for a red-carpet interview by my then employers at E!, Rourke informed the stunned reporter that he was displeased with my sarcastic jab at his tiny, dead pet. "Who's that guy who made fun of my dog? Joel McCrea, from *Talk Soup*. If you see him, tell him he's gonna get a slap in the face." The slap never amounted to anything of consequence, but I still wait—every night, under a lone streetlamp, gripping a white carnation and a pet-bereavement card that reads, "I Am Sorry the Tiny Dog You Loved Had to Pass Away, Mickey Rourke."

The fallout from Dead Dog–gate taught me some valuable lessons about celebrity feud protocol. Just like in jousting, there are rules of good form to be observed. For one, don't make a joke about a dead pet. That's kind of a dick move. Secondly, size up your target

---

[7] A Coton de Tuléar I received courtesy of *Gilmore Girls* star Lauren Graham, I believe as thanks for all the kissing we did in that Christmas movie.

beforehand. Is your would-be opponent someone who has trained as a professional boxer? And do they also believe that you are a long-deceased actor from the 1950s who now inexplicably hosts a talk show round-up series that went off the air in 2002? If either scenario is true, move on to another target.

What that experience really taught me—and which I pass along to you—is the concept of "punching up." This is a phrase that has grown in prominence, thanks to two things: people becoming overly sensitive about jokes, and the shady, underground world of MMA dwarf fights.[8] In this case, "punching up" means confronting someone who is above you—either in career stature or social influence. For me, "punching up" specifically meant humiliating a bona fide screen legend.

It was the night of the White House Correspondents' Dinner. If you'll remember from a recent chapter, I hosted this event—flinging out sarcastic barbs at every Tom, Dick, and Barb in the room. But I saved my harshest, most pointed jokes for Bob. That's right:

Mister Bobert De Niro.

I knew De Niro would be in attendance, and in order to space out all my material about then speaker of the house John Boehner's orangeness, I decided to zero in on a big, famous target. I would initiate a celebrity feud with Robert De Niro—by zinging him with a smart-ass comment *but good.*

Here's the joke I told: "Legendary actor Robert De Niro is here tonight. I don't do a De Niro impression, but I do an impression of his agent." I then mimed answering a phone, desperately barking,

---

[8] You should see that octagon. Adorable!

"He'll do it!" The joke got a warm, appreciative groan—so I knew it had struck a chord with the audience.[9]

I ran into De Niro at one of the after-parties, and he was actually very nice about the slight. "You had to do it," he told me.[10] "You had to—I woulda done it." Setting aside the confusing scenario he was suggesting—in which he, Robert De Niro, tells a scathing joke about himself to another Robert De Niro in the audience—I was still relieved. But also crestfallen. De Niro turned out to be remarkably cool about my taking a verbal dump on his entire career—which meant that my attempt to start a high-stakes celebrity feud had utterly failed.[11]

What I wish had happened was this: Robert De Niro, imposing titan of cinema, would clap me on the shoulder—too roughly to be considered friendly—and tell me that I offended him "a li'l bit." And then he would point me down an alley, where there were supposedly some free coats I could try on. "They're just in there. Go ahead . . . go ahead," he'd murmur, his lower jaw tightening. And I'd scamper off saying, "I gotta go, Jimmy! Henry's all whacked out on cocaine again and I think he's sleeping with that whore Janice Rossi!" It would've been glorious.

A few months later, Katie Couric interviewed De Niro and asked him about my joke. This is when the cracks began to show. "It hurt my feelings a li'l bit. A li'l bit," the classic screen tough guy whimpered. And with that, my celebrity feud with Robert De Niro was

---

[9] Unlike most of Robert De Niro's films since the late nineties.

[10] He does a *great* De Niro!

[11] Much like *The Adventures of Rocky & Bullwinkle, Righteous Kill,* and *Dirty Grandpa.*

back on, with a vengeance . . . until he invited me to speak at a dinner in his honor, because as it turned out, he was actually amused by
my insulting him. He is a complicated man, that Robert De Niro.
One moment, he's whining about mean jokes at his expense, and the
next, he's begging for more. I guess he just likes punishment, much
like those who have watched any Robert De Niro movie released
since 2002.[12]

Shortly thereafter, I got invited to yet another event with De Niro
in attendance—a dinner on behalf of a luxury watch company. You'll
see—once you become famous, you get invited to all sorts of wrist-
watch dinners. There's free food, free booze, and free watches. But
on that night, I would only be feasting upon one thing: an intense,
completely fabricated animosity toward Robert De Niro. Also, I had
a Caesar salad.

I had been invited to emcee this event, which, for me, would in-
volve ten minutes of bragging about the watch I was given and then
seizing the chance to take some potshots at the elites of culture and
finance who were also there because they, too, like free stuff. My
hosts for the dinner were a bit nervous that I would tease Robert De
Niro, but I assured them I would be completely respectful, saying,
"It's okay—me and that sack of shit go way back." I could hear them
just frantically blinking in reply on the other end of the phone.

Onstage, I said, "Mr. De Niro, why do you keep allowing me to
attend these things? I can't figure it out. I made a joke at your expense at the White House Correspondents' Dinner. Then you invited
me to an event in your honor, where I insulted you *again*. And here

---

[12] Like *Grudge Match*, where the grudge was against fans of quality cinema.

we are, together once more—engaged in this strange, emotionally charged dance. I insult you in public, you pretend to laugh, then you invite me to another event. When are the two of us just gonna fuck and get it over with?"

And then something magical happened: De Niro jumped to his feet and started heckling me. It was all a put-on, performed in a room full of about two hundred people, which means that, technically, I costarred in one of Robert De Niro's most well-attended comedies of the last five years. It was great.

Moments later, I posed for some photos with him—and here's why Robert De Niro is officially the coolest guy ever. As numerous photographers barked at us, snapping dozens of photos, De Niro just stood next to me smiling pleasantly while under his breath he repeatedly murmured, "Fuck *you*, fuck *you*, and fuck *you*" to all the cameras. You simply haven't lived until you've heard Robert De Niro cheerfully tell someone to fuck off in person. It's one of my most cherished career memories.

My dickish, ballsy move to engage in a feud with Robert De Niro took a lot of sack. But it was a gamble that paid off—because I stood up to a legend and was rewarded for my calculated insolence. And although I have taken a lot of shots at Mr. De Niro, his impact on cinema cannot be overstated. He will be forever remembered for his indelible performances in such classic films as . . . uh . . . wasn't he in . . . that one, with . . . *holy shit*. He's done it. He's finally done it. After years of forgettable appearances in dreck that is beneath him, Robert De Niro has completely wiped out any trace of his worthwhile contributions to the art of screen acting.

Wait a minute. He used *me* as an unwitting pawn in some sick game. He manufactured this drama from the get-go! It was in front of me all along! "You had to do it," he told me. "I woulda done it . . . *I woulda done it . . . I woulda done it . . . I woulda done it . . . I woulda done it . . . I woulda done it . . .*" He manipulated me into publicly mocking him—by systematically choosing to trade in his reputation for all those cash-grab acting roles! Then he shrewdly lay in wait for a sarcastic comedian to take the bait. That desperate comic's insults would net De Niro some sympathy and set him up for an even more lucrative comeback in non-shitty films! His plan is stunning in its simplicity.

How dare you, sir! I thought we were casual acquaintances! Remember that time you murmured obscenities at all those photographers alongside me? That was our special thing we did! And now it's been made cheap and disreputable. Well played, Bobert De Niro. This feud is officially back on. I'll see you on the set of *Spy Kids 5*!

The co-star of *Analyze That* poses with acclaimed actor Joel McHale.

Sometimes, your celebrity feuds won't lead to a long, exhausting back-and-forth of verbal abuse with no clear victor. Like in every good drama, there is a point where the events must lead to a thrilling, intensely realized physical climax.[13] And so it must be with *your* eventual celebrity feuds. For every dozen Mickey Rourkes, blithely threatening to bash your face the next time you never see each other in person ever again, there is that one instance where your quarry will tire of your unflattering impersonations during talk show appearances—and will resort to physical violence. In my experience, more often than not, that quarry has been septuagenarian comedy legend Chevy Chase.

As related in an earlier chapter,[14] I had my share of tussles with Chevy during the production of *Community*. I'm not saying I didn't necessarily deserve it. Chevy Chase had been a huge influence on a lot of people in my generation, and so I showed my respect and deference in the only way I knew how: by teasing him, and getting him to say ridiculous things, and making him chase a laser pointer.

So we were frequently at odds. He'd roughhouse with me in an effort to goad me into an aggressive form of ass-grabbery that I assume was how people related to each other in the seventies, when everyone was on cocaine. I would react in kind, usually bending his arm at a weird angle until someone insisted that I stop. This was a strange scenario—and not only because I was putting submission holds on the star of *Cops and Robbersons*. This was strange because

---

[13] With the exception of HBO's *Ballers*.
[14] We were so young then, you and I.

my knockabout attitude of confronting fellow celebrities had led one of them to actually fight back.

So when *you* are a successful, young-ish celebrity, and the time comes when you must physically fight Chevy Chase—and mark my words, that time will come—employ the following tips. They will save your life.

(For your safety, I have reproduced a handy instructional pamphlet originally commissioned for the benefit of female and minority members of the *Community* cast and crew.)

JOEL McHALE'S
"HOW TO SURVIVE A CHEVY CHASE ATTACK"

STAY PREPARED

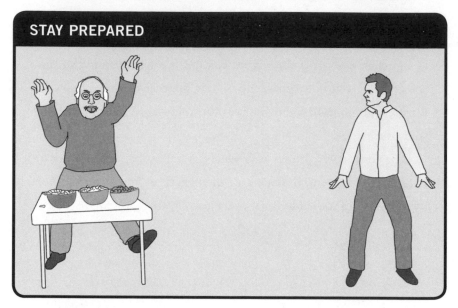

If you suspect a Chevy Chase is in the area, make some noise to alert him to your presence. If he approaches, pretend to be reading your script. Chevy Chases normally feed in the late morning hours, so be most wary near the craft services tent.

IF CHARGED BY A CHEVY CHASE . . .

Utilize any one of the following field-tested techniques to halt his progress, and subdue him until he can be tranquilized. I recommend you start with a two-gallon dose of tranquilizers and go up from there if he appears to be enjoying it.

"THE 'UNDER THE RAINBOW'"

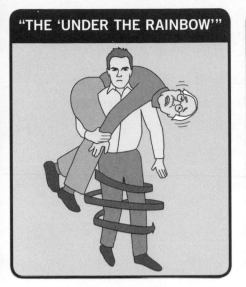

Crouch low, and while the Chevy Chase is confused, throw him onto your shoulder to perform a helicopter spin until he is so dizzy he begins to weep openly.

"THIGHS LIKE US"

Years of comical pratfalls have left the Chevy Chase's once-dense thighs and femurs particularly susceptible to pain. While he growls at you to "horse around with him," drop to one knee and bury both of your elbows into his thighs. You can then easily roll the Chevy Chase onto his back.

"THE DR. ROSEN-PENIS"

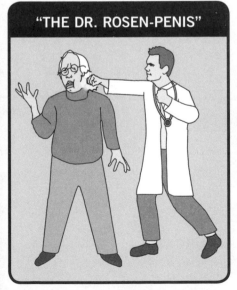

Dress like a doctor and approach Chevy. "You doing my old bits back at me?" he will bark, and while he is distracted, you can punch him in the face.

YOU CAN CALL ME 'OW'"

Wield any nearby portable item—like an overhead projector or legendary singer-songwriter Paul Simon—to knock Chevy Chase off his balance. While he is weakened, tell him you think women are just as adept at performing comedy as men. This will stagger him, and you can go in for a simple submission hold.

I trust you now feel adequately prepared to take your seething sense of entitlement and your gnawing career envy, and put them both to good, positive use! Now get out there, and *get feuding*![15]

---

[15] Make sure it's with someone of your same gender and race, otherwise it could be construed as a "hate crime." This is a vital point that I probably should not have relegated to a footnote.

IT GREW BACK ALL BY ITSELF

DEBUNKING THE NASTY RUMORS THAT
WILL FOLLOW YOU EVERYWHERE

I f you have adhered to the straightforward lessons of the previous chapters, you will wake up one morning (or, more likely, around two a.m., due to a recurring night terror where Matthew Lillard steals all your acting roles) and realize that you are officially rich and famous. You worked, and you suffered, and you hosted something called *The Best of the Worst Dating Show Moments* for some reason you do not remember,[1] and now—despite the embarrassment of that last thing—you have attained your goal.

And how do you know that your goal of fame, wealth, and celebrity has been achieved? Because you received the official notarized certificate proclaiming you an actual member of the Entertainment Industry's Upper Echelon—a vaunted cabal that consists of only the most respected and well-compensated members of show business. No one ever mentions this certificate, since this physical proof of

---

[1] Oh, now you remember: the reason was five hundred dollars cash.

your celebrity is a closely held Hollywood secret, and also because when somebody hands it to you, at your thirty-fifth birthday party, everyone laughs.

But I assure you that this honor is very real—and to prove my point, I will now risk estrangement from the celebrity community by including a facsimile of said certificate:

Certificate of Recognition

This Is To Certify That

Joel McHale

is hereby inducted into the ranks of the

Entertainment Industry's Upper Echelon

★ Joel McHale ★
Certificate is not binding unless signed by recipient

Now it's official! HaHa!!

HAPPY BIRTHDAY, JOEL!

The author's official certificate of celebrity, reprinted here at great personal risk to himself.[2]

---

[2] I will admit: As a freshly minted celebrity, I was suspicious. I had never heard of this certificate, and my friends and family members all knowingly giggled, as if this, along with the five-dollar bill that was taped to the certificate, was some kind of "birthday joke." I chuckled, because I was uncertain and didn't want to offend. Later, I examined the certificate closer, and after much internal debate, I decided that it was obviously a fake. The *real* certificate, I concluded, was probably locked in a vault in Beverly Hills. I relaxed and soon fell into a peaceful slumber, content in

Official documentation aside, how else can you tell that you are finally a famous and successful celebrity? Simple: People keep saying stuff about you.

In fact, the very definition of the word "celebrity" is "a person who people keep saying stuff about."[3] So that's how you *really* know you have made it: you will have morphed from a real person, with thoughts and feelings, into a symbol. You're totemic and mythic— like the Egyptian god Anubis. And just like Anubis, you will have to deal with people writing nasty rumors about you on the Internet.

Every morning, I Bing myself. Usually in the shower. I turn on my waterproof iPad and enter "jeol mchlea" into the search field, then Bing helpfully autocorrects to whatever the actual spelling of my name might be, and *boom*—I am given up-to-the-minute news on myself.[4]

All celebrities do this. Whether they have a Google Alert or an Ask Jeeves bookmark, every single famous person routinely verifies their own famousness via the Internet. Rumor has it that Gwyneth Paltrow has a French pig that has been trained for the sole purpose of conducting web searches about her. The pig waddles into the room, presses its wet snout against the keyboard of a laptop, and

---

the knowledge that I was, from that point forward, every inch the celebrity. (Or centimeter, when working on projects outside the US.) Later, when I mentioned this certificate to other celebrities, they acted as though they had never heard of such a thing. "I've never heard of such a thing," Chris Evans laughed at me. And then I laughed, because it did seem sort of ridiculous. And then I laughed even harder, imagining the Joel McHale and Chris Evans official celebrity certificates hanging out together, in that mysterious vault in Beverly Hills. And before long, I couldn't even remember why I was laughing.

[3] At least, it is in the handwritten, heavily illustrated dictionary that my wife made for me.

[4] Or in the case of Bing, up-to-the-week.

boom—Gwyneth has instant access to whatever weird rumors people are posting about her.[5]

If, upon reading the previous paragraph, you have not already set this book aside in order to immediately perform an Internet search on yourself, then guess what? You are not self-obsessed and solipsistic[6] enough to be famous. But don't worry—we can fix that.

"GAY HAIR WIFE HEIGHT DIVORCE"

How to Gauge Public Opinion of Yourself Through a Cursory Internet Search

Step 1: Have a Good "Famous Person" Name

If your name is a common one—like Will Smith, Jennifer Lawrence, or Common—then it will take hours to sift through the search results, and you'll only be faced with the reality that you are merely one of several billion people on the planet. And you're famous—you don't need to waste your time thinking about stuff like that!

So, if necessary, change or alter your name to stand out. Lots of celebrities do it! Michael Keaton was actually born Michael Douglas.[7] Samuel Jackson added an "L.," and Peapo Bryson had to surgi-

---

[5] Like that one about the spider monkey she trained to update her Netflix queue.

[6] A fancy word that also means "self-obsessed." In my wife's handmade dictionary, there's a picture of me next to it! Yay! I'm everywhere.

[7] A name he couldn't use professionally, as it was being used by talk show host Mike Douglas.

cally have his or her second "p" turned upside-down just to become legendary R & B singer *Peabo* Bryson.

Step 2: To Broaden Your Horizons, Narrow Your Results

If you're famous enough,[8] then there will be a lot of insane stuff about you on the Internet. There will be Croatian fan pages, incredibly detailed erotic fiction, countdown clocks to whenever you turn eighteen, and entire Tumblr pages with images of your head superimposed onto the torsos of nude cartoon characters. This is all very standard, incredibly flattering material—but it will only get in between you and what you are really looking for: the latest rumors about you. So include details in your search, perhaps based on an event that you are secretly afraid someone may have witnessed. Samples include "joel mchale hit and run," "joel mchale dine and ditch," and "joel mchale crunch 'n munch."[9]

Step 3: Hit "Enter"

I have to include this step. We are talking about celebrities, after all.

Step 4: Duck and Cover, Because Here Come the Truth Bombs

You will be bombarded with search results that may be unpleasant to read, like "joel mchale not funny," "joel mchale comedic hack," and "joel mchale fiddle faddle."[10] But remember the old adage "There

---

[8] And at this point in the book, you really should be.
[9] For the record, I was buying Screaming Yellow Zonkers.
[10] That time, I was buying Poppycock.

is no such thing as bad publicity."[11] Buck up! Because if somebody is searching for details on your relationship status, snack purchases, hat choices, comedic ability, or bikini bod, then at the very least, someone is thinking about you. And the more people that are thinking about you, and wondering why you simply don't purchase Cracker Jack, then the more famous you are!

Step 5: Accept Your Fallibilities, and Then Have Them Debunked by Your Publicist

When you become a celebrity, people will write things about you that are patently false. You're only human,[12] so every once in a while, the negative stuff will actually sting a bit. Journalists will claim that you were rude, paparazzi will claim that you don't like being called a "panda fucker" in public, and waiters will claim that you punched them. Whether or not these accusations are true is not important, because they are most definitely *not* true. This is why you hired a publicist in the first place[13]—to remind friendly journalists that the rest of their peers are muckraking liars. And so is that TMZ photographer, and that zoo employee, and that waiter.

Step 6: Close Your Laptop and Make Sure It Is Charging for Tomorrow's Search

If you forget to do this last step, then when your phone chirps at seven a.m. with a message from your publicist about the panda you

---

[11] And that other adage about there being no such thing as a clichéd adage.
[12] Sort of.
[13] Oh, step 4.1 is "Hire a Publicist."

had sex with,[14] you will not be able to quickly research how far the story has spread. And you will become so enraged by your own forgetfulness that you will most likely punch the next waiter you encounter.

Some rumors can survive the most bloodthirsty of publicists and the crispest of hush money. Rumors, in this way, carry more power than the actual truth—because rumors can become legends. Just ask Paul Bunyan. He wasn't *actually* a giant lumberjack who could fell trees in a single chop. He was just a regular, non-wood-chopping giant who ran a gigantic bed-and-breakfast. One day, a guest complimented Bunyan on his B & B's well-stocked kindling pile, inferring that Paul must have done all that chopping himself. And there you go. Legend![15]

In these scenarios, when you are dogged by a horrible rumor,[16] you must pivot—and use that publicity to your advantage. You can do this by indirectly admitting to the truth and then (a) capitalizing on the notoriety, (b) using this potential embarrassment to give the false impression you are relatable, or (c) talking about it in a circuitous, overly descriptive way, so as to add to the overall page count of your inevitable self-help book. But however you handle this pesky rumor, you *must* tackle it head-on—especially if the rumor has something to do with your own actual head.

Which brings me to my next point.

For as long as I have been recognizable, people have also been

---

[14] "We need to get out in front of this thing, Joel. And no, I do not mean the panda."
[15] Also, Babe the Blue Ox was nothing more than a massive blue *steer*. How do these things get started?!
[16] Usually about how you run a dogfighting ring.

recognizing my hair. This is natural, since my hair is located right above my face, on top of my inconsistent amount of forehead. There have always been rumors about my hair. And since you paid for this book,[17] I will respect the social contract between tell-all author and tell-all purchaser, and tell-you-all the truth.

Purely for illustrative purposes, here are two photos—taken, at random, from different points in my career:

Me in 2014   Me, time indeterminate

For years, I have had to read (or, more specifically, have read *to* me) rumors about my hairline. These proclamations, from self-congratulatory Internet photo sleuths, have included "That isn't his hair," "That dude used to have less hair," "He suddenly has more hair—what's up with that?" and "Joel McHale had a hair transplant."

---

[17] Presumably. Please don't tell me you're one of those deadbeats who "borrows books from friends."

And I can say, honestly, that none of those statements is true. Let's analyze their veracity, one at a time.

"That isn't his hair." FALSE. It *is* my hair. All of what is currently on top of my head is actually my hair. You might think that's an evasive way to phrase my explanation. It is not—but I'll play along. Let's pretend, solely for the sake of argument, that it *is* a hairpiece. If so, then I would have purchased that hairpiece, and therefore, it would still, technically, be *my hair*.

"That dude used to have less hair." FALSE. I will allow *this*: All of us—every human being on Earth—used to have less hair. It was when we were babies. So I guess you're insinuating that every infant, throughout human history, has "had something done" or "gotten plugs" to achieve the natural hair that they possess later in life. Singling me out as "that dude" suggests that I was the only baby who was once partially bald, and that is patently untrue.

"He suddenly has more hair—what's up with that?" First of all, this is phrased like a half-assed question. Who do you work for, a middle-school newspaper? Anyway, your dumb statement/question is nevertheless FALSE. Nothing that has ever transpired on my scalp—and I'm not admitting anything here—has ever happened "suddenly." The growth, theoretical recession, and surprise migration of my individual hair follicles all would have happened—if they happened at all—at a normal human rate. Moreover, I take issue with your use of the word "suddenly." That denotes the passage of time, and the very nature of time—

something that can be affected by individual memory and experience—is subjective. Therefore, your whole stupid hypothesis sucks, and any theoretical physicist would agree with me.[18]

"Joel McHale had a hair transplant." FALSE. I had two.

So what have we learned? Hopefully, that most rumors are simply not true. And the ones that are true are merely the result of a business decision. So, me telling you—in a roundabout way—that I paid a lot of money to have some hair that was already on my head moved to other parts of my head, is not a purposefully convoluted evasion. Rather, this is something that I am sort of admitting to, in an attempt to make a completely rational point about my successful career and the role my hair plays in it.[19]

Sure, I could have trusted solely in my own talent, charisma, and work ethic to build a career. But why depend on fleeting, inconsequential qualities like those when a simple thirty-thousand-dollar visit to Dr. Magic Scalp could tip the scales in my favor?

"But, Joel," you might be scoffing, "*lots* of beloved, attractive, famous leading men are bald." Sure, if you would classify a list of names that only includes Bruce Willis as "lots." The rest of the bald guys in Hollywood are character actors, and if I wanted to be one of those, then I wouldn't have subjected my body to all the stuff I described in chapter 15.

---

[18] Especially Stephen Hawking and his suspiciously lustrous mane of hair.
[19] "Pardon me, waiter? There's a hair in my roll. This is why I keep punching you."

History has proven that hair is very important. No one has ever followed a bald leader.[20] There's never been a bald US president—at least, not since wigs went out of fashion and we stopped giving our elected officials the option of painted portraits. Baldness—although an admirable artistic choice—is only ever associated with the two qualities of intensity and trying to murder Superman (typified by Lex Luthor and the lead singer of Midnight Oil).

My point is this: If you want someone to appear unstable, or intense, or as the villain in 1997's *Con Air*, you hire a bald guy. If you want someone to appear confident, or assured, or as the hero in 1997's *Con Air*, you hire a guy with a convincingly full head of hair.

So to control the trajectory of your career, take matters into your own hands. Or into the hands of whatever cosmetic surgeon is performing the procedure. Sure, okay. Let's take the example of my hair, yet again, since you pricks simply won't let that go.

Let us travel, through the veil of fantasy, into the world of the unknown as we examine some highlights from my acting career to see how very different things would have been if I had little to no hair . . .

---

[20] With the exceptions of Vladimir Lenin, Captain Jean-Luc Picard, Benito Mussolini, and Professor Charles Xavier. And two of those were the same guy!

Ted (talking teddy bear movie intended for adults—2012)

MY ACTUAL ROLE: Smarmy, sexually aggressive dickhead boss to Mila Kunis's character and romantic rival to Mark Wahlberg's character. I had no contact with the talking teddy bear, but I did meet him at the premiere.

MY THEORETICAL LESS-HAIR ROLE: I would instead have been cast in a nonthreatening, asexual role with no authority. I would have played an accident-prone valet parking attendant who gets his genitals stuck in a car door and is then mocked by the talking teddy bear as the car slowly rolls into traffic.

Deliver Us from Evil (movie about ghost cops or something—2014)

MY ACTUAL ROLE: Cool, renegade, adrenaline-junkie sidekick. This is a tricky one, since my character was mostly defined by his backward baseball cap. But the audience instinctively *knew* that there was hair under the character's hat. That's what made him both cool and a renegade—he didn't wear the cap to hide a bald head, he wore it to overcompensate for not being Eric Bana.

MY THEORETICAL LESS-HAIR ROLE: One scene as the Sandwich-Eating Coroner, and a single line of dialogue: "You think this is the work of *ghosts*, Detective?"

Community **(TV series— 2009–2015; movie released on streaming-only platform—2018; ill-advised reboot—2021–22)**

MY ACTUAL ROLE: The arrogant, attractive, self-obsessed lawyer having sexual relationships with women twenty years his junior. That description alone tells you right away that Jeff Winger is obviously the likable, relatable hero of a cult sitcom. But he was also defined by his wonderful hair, which was also *my* wonderful hair.

MY THEORETICAL LESS-HAIR ROLE: Deprived of my hair, I would never have been cast as rakish, thick-maned Jeff Winger. The role would have gone to that bastard Matthew Lillard, and *he* would be writing this book, the content, title, and cover design of which I can only assume would be slightly different.

O nce again, if I *had* opted for two hair transplant procedures, you have to admit: that would have been a very astute business decision—a wise investment in both my career and my scalp.

And if it's something you still want to talk about—well, great. Because every time you do, my hair just naturally gets thicker, while my wallet grows fatter.[21]

Here we see the author during one of his favorite leisure-time activities: riding a Jet Ski face-first into the gale-force wind produced by an industrial turbine. So, suck it.

---

[21] Until I have to pay to make the first thing happen again.

BECAUSE YOU KIND OF EARNED IT

A FIELD GUIDE TO THE BENEFITS, PERKS, AND ENTITLEMENTS SOCIETY BESTOWS UPON THE FAMOUS

Many self-help guides will tell you that a key step toward self-enrichment is using your energy and talents to help others. But that misses the main points of self-enrichment: *self* and *rich*. Helping other people sounds great, in theory. But if *I* focus only on the needs and welfare of others, then who is looking out for *me*? Some other person? That seems like a shady deal.

Think about it in your own life: if *you* are only concerned with the betterment of other people, then who will worry about *you*?[1] My advice: Do your part for humanity by focusing on your own needs. Then, once you have enough wealth and free shoes, your fellow man will enjoy the positivity overslop that occurs as soon as you have satiated your deeply held need to acquire things.

---

[1] And by "you" in this sentence, I also mean "me."

Picture yourself as a bubbling, hot-cheese fountain at a wedding. You can only hold so much liquid cheese. At some point, you will overflow, and believe me—there will be plenty of other people, hungry for cheese, who will step forward to fill their crackers, toast points, suit pockets, and handbags with all the molten Gouda you can't contain. This is the history-proven concept of "trickle-down consumption," and I promise you that it really does work. A rising tide raises all boats, especially if that tide is the wake caused by my giant yacht.

I shouldn't have to explain how money works, and not simply because I don't actually know. You are in the process of becoming a hugely famous and successful person, even as you read this very book—that's why your fingers are tingling![2] So very soon, you will be up to your famous ass, and your successful ears, in money. And it will be wonderful. That's all you really need to know about monetary gain.

"*Tsk, tsk,*" the more sensitive of you might be clucking. "Money does not buy happiness, Joel." And my response would be this: money bought the material you used to cross-stitch that phrase on a sanctimonious throw pillow, and didn't that act of superiority make you happy? So, it's official—I'm right, and you and your pillow are wrong. Money can buy peace of mind, expensive vacations, unnecessary medical procedures, and cars for all those cousins you never knew you had.

"But can your money buy the sun, and the moon, and the stars?"

---

[2] It could also be the discounted ink used to print this book (yes, even the e-book version). If your tongue goes numb, call a doctor.

is probably your follow-up pillow, and my only response to that would be, "Grow up, hippie. I'll be over here, in my recliner that has a cup holder, watching a lunar eclipse in stunning HD resolution on my TV—which is also a motorcycle." Then I'd gun the engine, and my tele-cycle would spray mud all over you, the other hippies, and your haughty throw pillows. Pillows, I might add, that you are selling outside this imaginary Phish concert in exchange *for money,* you hypocrite![3]

I could go on about money, but we all understand its many benefits. And eventually, we will each learn about some of its occasional downfalls, usually when visited by the ghost of a former coworker on Christmas Eve.[4]

But as a celebrity, you will come to learn of the many nonmonetary benefits of your fame. Yes, even though you now have enough cash to choke a horse,[5] you will still be given many additional things: gifts, preferential treatment, special access, and more! This is one of the most unbelievable parts of being famous—all the free stuff. The best way to describe this phenomenon is that someone has given you a goose that routinely poops out golden eggs. But then you discover that the goose is actually a thick-necked Serbian bouncer named Bogdan, and he will be personally escorting you past all the velvet ropes and secret doors—to rooms filled with free sweaters! It's so amazing, you will decide to overlook Bogdan's ceaseless egg pooping.

---

[3] I'm sorry I yelled at you—I'm so drunk right now.

[4] For more about my thoughts on personal financial gain, please purchase a copy of *Thanks for the Money*—now available wherever books are sold!

[5] And then reimburse the horse's owner for their trouble.

Over the next few pages, consider me *your* Bogdan: a towering Serbian goose with an irritable bowel who is about to whisk you, dear reader, into the magical realm of celebrity perks!

SUBSECTION A: TALES OF THE GOLDEN TOTE BAG

Scoring Free Things from Corporations, Individuals, and Charitable Organizations

Once you are a big celebrity, it can be exceedingly difficult to lure you out of the house—either due to your need for privacy or because whenever you go out, you are certain that a CIA black helicopter is monitoring your every move. Event coordinators will be desperate for your appearance at their high-profile gala so that you will (a) promote their new product, (b) speak on behalf of their super-depressing charity, or (c) accept an Academy Award for Best Actor. And the only surefire way to coax shy and/or cripplingly paranoid celebrities into the open is a well-stocked gift bag.

Every big Hollywood event has its own opulent satchel of free things. At the Grammys, nominees and guests receive complimentary Bluetooth speakers, while at the People's Choice Awards, every attendee is given a People's Choice Award. The better, high-profile events will also feature an entire room, called a "gifting suite," that is lined with different booths, each staffed by wet-eyed product representatives eager to have you model their wares in public. These are like kiosks at the mall, only instead of selling you those remote-controlled mini- copters, they're trying to give you free hand lotion made from artisanal honeycombs.

My advice is this: Visiting the gifting suite is like going to the grocery store. Don't send your assistant when you're hungry, or you will be forced to text them every two minutes, as you remember new things that you want to eat. Pace yourself. Take it slow. Plus, if you stumble in there, as a newbie celebrity, and immediately grab two dozen solid brass iPhone cases, the product reps will all roll their eyes. And you need these people on your side, because—and I speak from experience—there is a "secret menu" of even *more* free stuff, available to you if you play your cards right.[6]

Once, on a lark—and as a test of the very limits of my celebrity-ness—I brought two unemployed writers into a gifting suite with me. Typically, this is frowned upon, as free luxury items are not to be wasted on the nonfamous; also, since these particular people weren't working, they would sincerely appreciate the free things, which automatically diminishes the value of the items. But I didn't care—I wanted to see how far I could go. I was drunk with power, and also the forty-times-distilled luxury vodka they handed out at the gifting suite entrance.

So, with one of these sweaty, nonworking, nonfamous writers in tow, I stormed up to a booth offering free accommodations at a four-star hotel in Bora Bora. "We would be more than happy to have you," I was told by the hotel representative. But I already knew that. What I *didn't* know was if I could finagle four free nights at an over-lagoon bungalow for my slovenly, sad-sack writer friend.

---

[6] Ooh—look! Playing cards made from whale baleen! Grab two packs!

"And this guy is gonna need one, too," I said, nodding happily to the booth rep, and her face turned whiter than Tahitian sand. I know the exact color of that sand because the pale, quivering, chubby writer showed me the photos he took *after I successfully scored him that trip*. So, when you are enjoying your gift bags, and your gifting suites, and your gift mints in the bathroom, remember that the best gift is one you pass along to someone in need—because you've already been to Bora Bora, and you and your wife couldn't work around the blackout dates anyway.

SUBSECTION B: MORE LEG ROOM THAN GOD

A Tantalizing Glimpse at How You Will Travel as a Famous Person

The average person dreads going to the airport. And I don't blame them. Air travel, for the upper-middle-class people who can actually afford it, is a carnival of horrors.[7] Sitting in a coach seat on a transcontinental flight is akin to being locked inside an overbooked sleep clinic where people are actively encouraged to bring their own burritos. I don't have to tell you how awful air travel is—odds are, 38 percent of you are on a plane at this very moment.

Personally, I don't dread going to the airport. And soon—as a wealthy, famous person—you won't either. Because for us, our vacation starts the moment the trip actually begins![8]

---

[7] One of those carnivals of horrors where you have to pay twenty-five dollars to check a bag.

[8] This is especially true if you are going on vacation.

Here now, I offer you a detailed look at how rich celebrities travel. You may want to refer back to this section as inspiration, to push you toward your eventual goals. Or, if your dreams of wealth and fame don't pan out,[9] you may consult this section when you need yet another reason to actively resent the wealthy.

Now boarding—McHale Airlines flight 312, with service to Luxury City, Comfort Town, and Gosh You Spoil Me–ville!

CAR SERVICE—"Where to, mister? . . . Just kidding, that info was already provided by your assistant."

In your former (or current[10]) life, you had to take a cab, or bum a ride from a friend, or worse, *drive yourself,* just to get to the airport. Not anymore! Now a man in a suit will pick you up in a black SUV—and your white-glove, platinum-level travel experience will officially be under way! You will sit in comfort as you are plied with miniature bottles of water and strange magazines that can only be found inside livery service vehicles.[11]

AIRPORT ARRIVAL—The beginning of the end of your not enjoying air travel

Your driver (probably named Victor) will deposit you right at the curb. In some cases, he may even pick you up and lift you out of the car, to gingerly place you in front of your departing airline's check-in

---

[9] No refunds.
[10] See footnote 9.
[11] My favorite? *Livery Service Vehicle Magazine Monthly*!

area. This is what is known as "curbside service." You're a celebrity now, and there's no sense in expending unnecessary energy through the movement of your own muscles—let Victor do that for you.

This next part is crucial, as here is where you truly begin the wonderful process of being excluded from all the dumb crap that regular travelers must endure. Do not—I repeat, do NOT—go into the normal airport entrance. You're not a normal person anymore, so you don't need to travel in any normal ways. Look to the left of the regular airport entrance (which should now appear disgusting to you). There will be a nondescript door manned by a guy in a suit. You've probably never even noticed that guy before, and that's because, to the eyes of the normal traveler, he is *completely invisible*. This guy will greet you and usher you through the nondescript door. You do not need to worry about tipping or even acknowledging this man—in most cases, he is a robot, programmed only to facilitate comfortable travel for the wealthy.[12]

CHECK-IN—Where you don't prove yourself to security, *they* prove themselves to *you!*

As a celebrity, you waltz[13] through the nondescript door and up to the classiest, ritziest check-in kiosk that your formerly coach-traveling eyes have ever seen. Now, what I am about to say is not intended as a critique of your standard airport employees—but the lot of them are

---

[12] Asimov's fourth law of robotics: Never allow a human to pay for their own noise-canceling headphones.

[13] You will find the standard celebrity airport music is Strauss's *Blue Danube*, and therefore waltzing is just irresistible.

sullen, vindictive vest jockeys. Standing in stark contrast to their un-derpaid counterparts are the celebrity kiosk airport check-in people: twinkly eyed, rosy cheeked, and genuinely happy to see you.

Maybe you are one of those people currently enrolled in the De-partment of Homeland Security's "TSA Pre-Check" program—that thing where you pay a bunch of money to get fingerprinted and then are allowed to skip the longer security line. "I don't even have to take my belt off," you might be bragging, as if that compares to the triple-diamond-level travel experience that I'm about to describe.

Yes, the TSA Pre-Check feels great . . . if you're a *normal* person. But it's actually a scam, intended to dissuade aspiring celebrities from trying harder. "This is good enough," the Pre-Check program is softly whispering to you. And you may be tempted to believe that. "B-b-but . . . they don't make me remove my dumb Sony Vaio laptop from my sad JanSport backpack," you may reply. That's cute. As a celebrity—traveling at service levels well above this precious Pre-Check—you won't have to remove your belt, either. It will already be seductively stripped from you by the entire airline industry, just so they can more thoroughly please you.

Once your ID and security clearance are verified—usually with a cursory glance at your IMDb credits, followed by a knowing wink—you are personally ushered into a private elevator . . . that exits where? That's right—*directly in front* of the TSA Pre-Check line.

Savor this delectable moment, because you will be permitted to do something that has been frowned upon since kindergarten: *cut-sies*. The TSA employee will wave you in front of the Pre-Check trav-elers, who—just moments prior—were feeling all high and mighty as they breezed past the line of normals. Sorry, Pre-Checkers, but there's still an alpha predator on this savannah, and he needs to get on the plane before his bowl of warmed cashews gets cold.

AIRPORT LOUNGE—The bar where everybody knows your name, because you show them your lounge access card upon arrival

Since your driver, special check-in treatment, and vice-presidential-level security access have made you two hours early for departure, you need a place to go to prepare for your flight.[14] You are now in the lounge, and it is glorious—mostly because here, you are not exposed to the typical airport gate experience: dozens of people sitting on the floor, clustered around the one working electrical outlet as they fight over the remains of a stale cinnamon roll.[15]

BOARDING—You've got a Golden Ticket! (To sit on a plane for four hours)

Like any passenger, you should arrive at your gate with enough time to board. But this isn't for fear of missing your flight. Legally, airline pilots are forbidden from closing the cabin doors until all celebrities and rich people are on board and enjoying their pre-takeoff foot rubs. The *real* reason you need adequate time is to soak in every aspect of the boarding process. Previously, in your nonfamous, unwealthy past life, this part of air travel was just another over-priced slog.

---

[14] By drinking two vodka-sodas and ingesting half a sleeping pill. If it's a morning flight, you may opt for two screwdrivers instead. Or four beers. Whatever. The important thing is to get drunk.

[15] Animals. Fucking *animals*.

But now, as a prized member of first class, you can:

- Board the plane before the babies, elderly, and US service-persons!
- Bask in the gloriously hot fumes of envy wafting your way from jealous coach passengers!
- Joke about bombing the plane![16]

Sure, you are still essentially being treated like cattle—but in this scenario, you're a *really spoiled cow*. Like one of those Japanese Wagyu cattle that are given beer and deep-tissue massages.

THE MIRACLE OF FLIGHT (and the miracle of warm chocolate-chip treats while in flight)

Unlike that quitter Daedalus and his whiny kid Icarus, there are no heights to which you cannot fly. You are in first class now, where simply everything is free—the drinks, the food, and the never-ending sense of entitlement. Here's a pro-tip from me, an ace traveler: have someone book you on a newer-model aircraft, so that you can (a) enjoy one of those personal first-class "sleeper pods" and (b) ensure you're riding in a plane that won't comically split in half somewhere over Nebraska.

Now that you're slouching, semiconscious, in your first-class seat-bed, prepare to be babied like never before![17] Prior to takeoff,

---

[16] Unless the air marshal or flight attendants are within earshot.
[17] Even more than that time when you were an actual baby.

you'll be offered coffee, tea, and juice. You will opt for the alcohol, and lots of it. Don't worry—the odds of your being asked to help land the plane are extremely slim![18] So drink up, and start to watch one of the *Captain America* movies, since all of them are available for complimentary viewing on every domestic airline flight ever.

Soon, due to the opulent comfort of your first-class butt-nest—and due to the alcohol and other treats (*cough, cough*—sleeping pills),[19] you will be whisked away to dreamland. And yes, slumbering through the entire flight may seem to be a waste of your plush travel experience. You could argue that, in unconsciousness, virtually all plane rides are the same. But that's merely logic, and logic is the domain of the pathetic and the desperate (i.e., people seated in coach). In first class, your slumber will be radically improved by the knowledge that at least forty rows of miserable travelers are staring at the back of your head and trying to make it explode with their thoughts.

At this point, after I have spent more pages of this book describing air travel than I have both my marriage and the birth of my children combined, you may be wondering, "What gives? Why not just fly via private jet, hotshot?" Simple—because I have done that before, and, while glorious, private jet travel is simply not as enjoyable as flying in a situation with multiple class levels. What's the point of being Billy Zane if you can't be aware that broadly drawn Italian

---

[18] Sometimes the captain will invite you into the cockpit, but usually this is just for some humorously staged "Joel McHale forcibly took over the plane!" photos, to be posted on the pilot's Facebook page.

[19] Actually, you better take something for that cough, too. Here—have a sleeping pill.

and Irish stereotypes are languishing down in steerage? I am reminded of the old saying "If a tree falls asleep while traveling in absolute luxury, but no normal people are around to witness it, does it still make the tree feel superior?"

BACK TO EARTH (stupid, normal, non-plush Earth— where most cookies are not free)

All wonders must cease, and soon after your aircraft kisses the tarmac, you must awaken and deplane. After four hours of luxury travel, your arrival can be quite a shock to the system—which is why more alcohol will be offered to you, and then imbibed by you, in the last twenty minutes of the flight. Woozy from your nap,[20] with a belly full of warm chocolate-chip cookies,[21] you step from the aircraft—and immediately slump into one of those wheelchairs reserved for old people. "It's okay, that's the *Soup* guy," a flight attendant will whisper, and a volunteer will quietly wheel you outside. I like to use this time to prepare myself for a bracing arrival back to the cold, hard, slightly less pampering real world. If the airport is too loud for you to properly reflect, then just wait until the courtesy limo ride to your five-star hotel.

---

[20] And those painkillers you thought were sleeping pills.

[21] You have just discovered the one loophole to my diet plan (the Joel McHale Patented Three-Step Process): any foodstuff consumed while an aircraft is climbing toward, or descending from, its final cruising altitude does not count.

SUBSECTION C: THE FIVE PEOPLE
YOU MEET IN HEAVEN

A First-Person Account of the Opening Night of Heaven, Las Vegas's Hottest New Nightclub

When you're famous, people will ask you to show up at the openings of various restaurants, attractions, and bars. The primary reason for this is to get photos of you, the celebrity, standing against a flat white backdrop that is covered in product logos—a few of which may even be for the actual restaurant, attraction, or bar in question. But part of the deal is that you have to go inside for even more photos of you, simulating enjoyment of the restaurant, attraction, or bar. This is a laborious, time-consuming part of your job—but it is also how you can discover what free stuff lurks inside.

I don't attend most of these events anymore, since there are already thousands of hours of footage of me standing against a green screen, and any interested parties can just license that footage and superimpose me into the indoor skydiving attraction they have decided to open. The last time I went to one, it was a glitzy bacchanal that commemorated the unveiling of the Las Vegas nightclub Heaven.[22] Your experience at these events—once you are famous enough to be whisked past the throngs of eager non-celebrities waiting in line for a chance to see you pose with a bottle of alcohol—will be re-

---

[22] Soon after, it was rebranded as "Criss Angel's Purgatory," and now it's home to a Cirque du Soleil show featuring the music of the Spin Doctors.

markably similar to mine. These are the Five People You Meet in Heaven.

Sebastian—The bouncer in Heaven. Sebastian's rough-hewn hands—like hamburger patties carved from stone—will be the first image you remember from your experience in Heaven. But those hands have a certain gentleness as they unclasp the velvet rope, softly take your elbow, and lead you past the gates. He will also escort you to the men's room, where you will be permitted to cut in line. "Hey!" a nonfamous clubgoer will bellow as you are ushered into the lavatory. "How come he gets to go before all of us?" Sebastian will then take one of his surprisingly tender paws and pin this man to the wall by his neck, rasping, "Because he's *better* than you!" Sebastian taught me humility, by displaying how other people will gladly throw my weight around for me.

Ashlee—Your personally assigned cocktail waitress in Heaven. There is a sadness beneath her clumsy attempts to up-sell you from the gratis bottle of vodka to one of the more opulent, top-shelf liquors available in Heaven. Ashlee sets a tray of mixers and an ice bucket in your booth, and you notice that the decorative sparklers throw deep shadows into the creases of her heavily made-up forehead and eyes. This is when you realize that Ashlee, like many of us, is wearing a mask—that life is a stage, and we are merely players. Anyway, I did eventually opt for the top-shelf stuff, but I insisted that Heaven's management cover the cost. From Ashlee, I learned the lesson of persistence.

Ashley—The Heaven attendee lured by bottle service. After standing in line for three hours, Ashley wants some of your free alcohol and a selfie with you for her Instagram page. Ashley is not interested in stories about your wife and children—she seems far more concerned with which filter will make her look skinniest. This truly is a person for whom the destination is more valuable than the journey. Also, Ashley's eyes are severely dilated and she is aggressively gnawing on a water bottle cap. From Ashley, I learned the value of self-awareness, and that the Mayfair filter is quite flattering.

Maxund Klo3rg3—The celebrity DJ in Heaven. His main responsibility is to ensure that clubgoers cannot have a conversation without inadvertently spitting on each other. As Maxund beseeched the crowd to put their hands in the air and wave them like they just do not care, I mused, "What does *he* care about?" It turns out, what Maxund cares about is your VIP standing within Heaven, and as such, he'd like you to tweet out a plug for his new book. Why does a celebrity DJ have a book? I wasn't paying attention. From Maxund, I learned the value of listening, and to a lesser degree, the value of putting one's hands in the air, to simulate a surrendering of personal cares.

Giancarlo—The bathroom attendant. His is the last face you see before departing Heaven. Giancarlo is wise beyond his years, and wise beyond his occupation of standing inches away from people as they relieve themselves. He seems to understand you better than anyone: when you require a hand towel, your opinions on recent shifts in weather patterns, and whether or not you're a "post-pee mint" kind of guy. You will see, in Giancarlo's basket of wadded-up singles, not a life wasted, but a life that is merely in progress. And you will give him a five-dollar tip, because— c'mon—the guy's office is a fucking bathroom. From Giancarlo, I learned perspective. So much, in fact, that I vow never to come to one of these soul-crushing club openings ever again.

SUBSECTION D: CAN I GET AWAY WITH MURDER *NOW*?

A Handy Chart That Matches Your Level of Fame with the Crimes Society Will Allow You to Commit Without Consequence

This is the goods. This is what you really want to know: "What can I get away with?"

First, a warning. Many assume that there exists an unspoken set of rules for the rich and famous—a tacit understanding with the rest of society that powerful, wealthy, and popular personalities will be permitted more transgressions than the average person. And I am here to tell you, *yes, that is entirely the case.*

However—and here's the warning part—there are limits. Before contemplating a crime, you must examine your own level of fame[23]

---

[23] And, if there's time, your own moral compass.

to better understand what ramifications you might face, if any. After consulting with numerous law enforcement and criminal justice experts, I present this handy chart. You may want to tear this section from the book to keep on your person at all times.[24] As a celebrity, you will inevitably realize that the desire to push against the boundaries of a civil society is simply too much to resist. You are now above the law . . . and the view is spectacular.

---

[24] And then immediately purchase a replacement copy of this book, because you just defaced it, you dirtbag.

JOEL McHALE'S CELEBRITY CRIME AND PUNISHMENT MATRIX

FAME LEVEL	CELEBRITIES INCLUDED	CRIMES PERMITTED
	Local newscaster; morning radio show sound effects technician; car dealership proprietor who appears in own advertisements	• petty theft • most forms of libel • price-gouging bottled water during natural disaster
	Lead singer for Mötley Crüe cover band; fat kid who fell off bike in YouTube video (minimum 300,000 views); actor who had sex with pie in late '90s comedy film; most podcasters	• public intoxication • light frottage • smuggling of water hyacinths
	Talking dog from canned baked beans commercial; reality show contestant who references their "heart on this journey"; Ryan Seacrest	• possession of illegal fireworks • fixing greyhound races • fraudulent use of 4-H Club emblem

(continued)

FAME LEVEL	CELEBRITIES INCLUDED	CRIMES PERMITTED
	Lead singer for Mötley Crüe; reality show contestant who isn't "there for the right reasons"; Internet celebrity (Vine excluded)	• mailing lottery tickets across state lines • vehicular manslaughter • excessive kick-starting of heart
	Half-clothed woman eating cheeseburger in national commercial; Texas high school quarterback; Bronson Pinchot	• online auction malfeasance • violation of primate quarantine laws • cyber-bullying
	Winner of MTV Movie Award for Best Kiss (or other award higher in stature than BAFTA); Heisman Trophy recipient; current Puppy Bowl champion; Mark Linn-Baker	• impersonating a police officer • drift-racing • drifter-smothering
	Oscar winner; Super Bowl MVP; musician whose fan base has a specific nickname; network television star (of at least two series that have reached syndication)	• false imprisonment • obstruction of justice • all the kinds of murder! • parking in a loading zone

* Note: Entire table applies only to Caucasians.

HAVING IT ALL, AND HOLDING ON TO IT FOR DEAR LIFE

EVERYTHING ELSE MY LEGAL REPRESENTATION WILL ALLOW ME TO PASS OFF AS "ADVICE"

Y ou did it! You followed every single one of my tips and guidelines, you glanced at the most eye-catching pictures, and you probably skimmed over the rest. Now take a deep breath and just exhale, my friend, because—*whew*—your journey is now complete . . . right?

Wrong! That was a trick, to test your Personal Fulfillment Level. I am sorry to say that if you currently feel some amount of inner peace and hard-earned satisfaction, then you are not yet prepared to be a true celebrity. The need to achieve, and succeed, and portray a morally compromised personal trainer on a Showtime series where every female character appears topless—that fire must be ever burning, like the pilot light on a success oven![1]

---

[1] Or that town in Pennsylvania where an underground coal fire has been burning for fifty years.

Being a wealthy celebrity isn't one of those cushy jobs, like construction worker, lawyer, marine biologist, or those people who look in my ears and ask what I've been eating.[2]

No, once you've landed the gig of ridiculously well-compensated famous person, you cannot just kick back and take it easy. This is a career that requires constant vigilance and troubling amounts of focus. You need to function like a lighthouse operator, or a bus driver, or a golf course groundskeeper who has crippling obsessive-compulsive disorder. Remember that if you don't keep a tight grasp on the responsibilities of your job, then you will crash the bus into the lighthouse, which will then collapse onto the viewing stands for the Women's PGA Championship at Locust Hill Country Club. I have seen it happen, people.

What you need to understand is that "having it all" also means "*maintaining* it all." As a successful celebrity, you are now responsible for the livelihoods of countless other people. This will add a certain amount of stress to your life and career. All your decisions—your creative choices, your business dealings, and your increasingly fevered conspiracy theories involving a Dutch crime organization called the Whispering Orchid—will impact these other people.

Sometimes, you'll want to just throw in the towel and slam the brakes on this whole celebrity thing. But, hey, you worked hard for that free towel, and your publicist yelled at a lot of people to get you those complimentary brake pads you just contemplated shredding. And what if the Whispering Orchid finds out about your plans? Don't act hastily. You are now responsible for all these others—the

---

[2] I think they're called . . . "drocktors"?

clingers, the well-wishers, and the people who don't actively wish you'd fall down a well. So what is to be done with them? Simple—organize them into several piles, for easier sorting.

I. THE BLOODTHIRSTY HORDE

Think of your professional representatives—those hardworking people who yell at other people on your behalf. What if you suddenly decided to pack it in, stop being a rich and famous actor, and just become a bearded, hermitic painter of impressionistic seascapes?[3] What would your agents do? Represent *other* wealthy, successful actors? Unlikely. As your talent agents have assured you on multiple occasions, you are the only client they truly care for. And if you suddenly tired of the constant executive nitpicking, nonstop media critique of your body, and psychological warfare of the entertainment industry,[4] your agents would simply shrivel up and die.

Hollywood agents are a unique and fragile species. They command 10 percent of your income, and they have to do that while only giving you 2 percent of their actual attention—and that is challenging. And because your professional career representatives have taken all their social cues from movies like *Wall Street* and *Boiler Room*, they are simply not cut out for some other industry—one where they may be expected to chew with their mouths closed and to refrain from constantly shouting, "You're crushin' it, bro!" These

---

[3] This is all I dream of.
[4] You could just retire to a small oceanside hamlet, get fat, and work on oil paintings of the coastline. It would be glorious.

agents helped you achieve your blazing-hot stardom,[5] and they are now your responsibility. Same goes for your publicists and manager.[6]

II. THE STEAMERS, BUFFERS, PLUCKERS, AND CLIPPERS

As a big-time celebrity, you now employ a veritable army of people who help maintain your physical appearance. These are the diligent, long-suffering folks who know exactly what your genitals are shaped like and how many sets of Spanx you require to fit into a Tom Ford dinner jacket,[7] so keep them happy.

The first time someone dressed me, and combed my hair for me, and applied glitter blush to my face, I thought, "This is absurd! I'm an adult man. How has it possibly taken *this* long for me to receive such treatment?" I was genuinely upset. I mean, why did I waste all that time as a child learning to bathe and groom myself if I was just gonna grow up to be a successful man who could have people do it for me—usually while I sleep? But there's no time to cry over a wasted adolescence. You're a professional actor and/or comedian, so your adolescence is *now*! And like true adolescents, your peers will judge your appearance harshly, so you really do need a personal style team. (Do what I did, and make them wear matching track-suits. Sure, they will complain about this, and other style teams will

---

[5] Once you did all the actual legwork.

[6] What's a manager? They're like an agent who does less work and just wants to hang out with you for some reason.

[7] This is just a hypothetical. I keep my shit tight—you know that.

make fun of them at the big Celebrity Style Team Winter National Competition, but it really is fun, fosters camaraderie, and helps you better identify your hairstylist in a poorly lit soundstage.)

You will need a personal dresser, like José, whose sole purpose is to take designer clothing and completely conceal all the body parts you have spent hours making aesthetically pleasing. Also, you will require the service of an ace makeup artist, like Pam, who will labor to conceal the blemishes, scars, and paint-huffing splatters that dot your skin.[8] And let us not forget the hairstylist, someone like Jade, who will keep your beautiful, flowing mane in tip-top shape.[9] If you suddenly stopped being a celebrity, then these dedicated, demure artisans would have to go work for one of the other famous people whom they are constantly complaining about while attending to your reasonable, incredibly detailed demands.

III. THE PROFESSIONAL BARNACLES

Let's not forget about your hangers-on. Now that you've become a celebrity, you have probably noticed these people lurking all around you. That dude over there, wearing a sideways ball cap, who says he can get you courtside seats? That budding restaurateur who just needs five minutes of your time to explain her "farm-to-table Lebanese Tex-Mex fusion concept"? Those two guys who have been ghostwriting your book? Craven, opportunistic hangers-on—all of

---

[8] Pam also has these illegal Japanese eyedrops that can make your sclera whiter than Anne Hathaway.

[9] Screw you—I already talked about this.

them! The trick here is that you may occasionally *need* these professional money sponges, so you must foster these connections; you never know when you're gonna need courtside seats, or a failed restaurant investment to use as a tax shelter, or two slobs to write a book for you. And while your coattails are now large and stylish enough[10] to accommodate all of them, you must be wary—these leeches can suck you dry, just like remoras on a great white shark.[11] Plus, you will need some leftover money for all the "favors" and "assistance" and "viable internal organs" that your relatives all suddenly need, now that you're rich and famous.

IV. THE FAMILIAL RELATIONS, LEGAL RESPONSIBILITIES, AND BLOOD HEIRS

Ugh, *these* guys. The worst—am I right? I kid my relatives and josh around with loved ones[12] because they are cut from the same freewheeling, sarcastic cloth that I am. They know that I only tease those whom I truly value in life, and that these jokes are just baseless exaggerations and not a reflection on our actual relationships.[13] Also, it is highly unlikely that they have even bothered to read this far, since I stopped mentioning them back in chapter 14.

---

[10] Thanks, José.

[11] I think that's what remoras do. I was only half watching that nature documentary, in order to show off my new TV—which I got for free, at a gifting suite.

[12] Especially that one kid Josh. He can really take a joke!

[13] You're all bleeding me dry! See? I was kidding right then. (No, I wasn't! [. . . Just messing with you—that was another classic McHale ribbing.] Help me! [Haha, jokes!])

These are the people who were really there for me in the early days of my career. Well, most of them. I'd say that around 37 percent of them were actually there for me—but those people were so supportive, and giving of their time and love, that they make up for those other slackers.

And when *you* are finally rich and famous, people like this will become your inner circle.

As the most trusted members of your coterie, these individuals will be there to nod knowingly when you complain about career slights, to catch any vases you throw at full-length mirrors, and to share in your moments of genuine triumph and creative satisfaction.[14] These are the warm, comforting laps and shoulders into which you will press your blubbering, tear-streaked face after you are once again overlooked by the Nickelodeon Kids' Choice Awards. And there's a trade-off, which is that—in exchange for their love and support—these loved ones and supporters will occasionally ask for favors.

What they need,[15] and the sincere-seeming excuses for it,[16] doesn't really matter. What matters is that, deep down, these people represent your last remaining connection to the old you—that bucktoothed, frizzy-haired dreamer from the wrong side of the tracks who, just months ago,[17] tumbled out of the back of a turnip truck and rolled to a stop at the gates of Hollywood. So it is vital that you

---

[14] Provided you have any. I mean, how much do you actually want out of this celebrity thing, anyway? Don't be greedy.

[15] An appearance at a wedding, some money to pay off a back-alley loan shark, etc.

[16] "We haven't seen you in years," "They're gonna take *my thumbs*, man," etc.

[17] Or six chapters ago, in "book time."

protect these people, because they have some very incriminating photos—of your buckteeth and your frizzy hair . . . they might even have one of you climbing into the back of that turnip truck without properly securing the tailgate. Keep these people close, because the entertainment industry is a cutthroat, knockabout business, and you will need true friends, trusted advisers, and people who are partial DNA matches who can kind of look like you.

So you can't simply give up on your own celebrity, because then all these loved ones and committed friends would suffer by proxy. They would be deprived of your backstage gossip, and your gift bag cast-offs, and the pleasure of your company or something.

V. THE UNWASHED MASSES

If you have made it through these other categories of people and thought—as many celebrities often do—that all of them can just suck it, then you could certainly give up. You could go to the head of the Celebrity Police, toss your piece and shield on his desk, and growl, "I'm done, Commissioner Gordon-Levitt. I'm taking my justice . . . to the streets."

But then you'd be forgetting about the most important, and also the most anonymous and relatively powerless, group of all—the audience. "Hey, wait a minute! That's me! You're talking about *me*!" you might be shouting into your book. First of all, settle down.[18] And secondly, yes, I realize it might be insulting to lump you all together

---

[18] And take a moment to wipe that fleck of spittle off your book or tablet screen.

into one big, undulating mass of yowling, farting humanity. Many of you are *not* indiscriminately loud and gassy blobs. In fact, I believe most of you to be intelligent, self-assured, and sexy consumers. I think of you—the people who have watched my TV shows, bought sidewalk pirated DVDs of my movies, and attended my stand-up comedy performances—as the customer. And the customer is always right.[19]

So even if, in your celebrity life, you fantasize about throwing it all away so you can open that combination yoga studio/plus-size consignment shop, you must keep the audience ever in your mind. You are a painter of light, a weaver of dreams . . . and what would the fans do without you? Probably fantasize about having sex with some other celebrity—and you can't allow that. After a while, they will run out of famous fantasy sex objects[20] and then might decide to put some work into their own lives, interests, and literal sex objects. And that is money being taken directly out of your pocket. Don't give up—you owe it to the frustrated, easily distracted[21] masses![22]

The previous pages were a detailed, needlessly Roman numeralized means of saying that, basically, people are gonna want stuff

---

[19] Unless they give this book a negative Amazon review for being "too smug."

[20] Especially if they get all the way down to the various Kevins (Connolly, James, et al.).

[21] Look—a bunny!

[22] Again, not *you* guys. You're cool.

from you. So how do you decide who gets your time and attention, and in what proportions? You could pit your loved ones, career representatives, and professional clingers against one another in a tournament where they must prove their dedication through gladiatorial combat. But your lawyer[23] will likely advise against this. There is an easier, more bloodless way to manage your time—a pie chart!

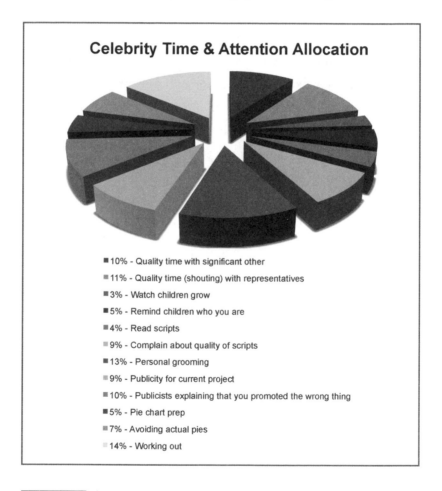

Celebrity Time & Attention Allocation

- 10% - Quality time with significant other
- 11% - Quality time (shouting) with representatives
- 3% - Watch children grow
- 5% - Remind children who you are
- 4% - Read scripts
- 9% - Complain about quality of scripts
- 13% - Personal grooming
- 9% - Publicity for current project
- 10% - Publicists explaining that you promoted the wrong thing
- 5% - Pie chart prep
- 7% - Avoiding actual pies
- 14% - Working out

---

[23] Another hanger-on!

With all these people pawing at your lapels and wheezing, "Me, me, what about me?!" it can be very distracting.[24] But you must be able to shift your attention—and the attention of as many other people as possible—back to what really matters: *you*!

BUT ENOUGH ABOUT ME

How to Cultivate the False Modesty That Will Allow You to Make Everything About You

Yes, that's right: false modesty. I am fucking great at it—probably one of the best, ever. And soon, you will be, too. In olden times, celebrities were rarely seen—in fact, just to catch a glimpse of a famous actor, you had to go to the cinematograph palace or the newsstand, or program the VCR Plus+ code for that evening's episode of *Entertainment Tonight*.

But now, with the advent of smartphones, and social media, and whatever future technology will make those first two things seem adorably outdated,[25] the public can see a famous person as easily as scaling the fence that surrounds that famous person's property. As a modern celebrity, you will have your own Twitter account, Instagram page, and Glurftr portal[26] with which to directly interface with your fans' faces. And relatability is *key*—that's what Ben

---

[24] Also, if people are frantically pawing and wheezing, you might all be sealed inside a car that has plunged into a canal. Check your surroundings to verify.

[25] My money is on Mind-Discs!

[26] Oh—you guys aren't on Glurftr yet? I guess I got one of the early, celeb-only invites.

Affleck told me one time, after we shared a tandem jetpack ride off the deck of his yacht. The public must never detect a whiff of the phoniness that wafts off you as a successful celebrity. They must smell that you are still one of them—and you can achieve this by embracing the three methods of false modesty.

Use a Tragic Celebrity Death to Your Advantage—There is nothing more heartbreaking than when one of our famous brethren passes away. It reminds us of our own fleeting mortality and, worse, foists a bunch of media and audience attention upon someone who can't even properly enjoy it. The deceased celebrity, now being honored with career retrospectives and heartfelt Facebook posts, can't capitalize on this publicity, mostly because of the whole being-dead-now thing. So that attention is just lying there, unused, in the form of genuine expressions of remorse and appreciation. Grab some of that for yourself!

Keep a well-maintained file of photos featuring you posing with legendary, aged, frail performers. Then, as soon as those celebrities shuffle off this mortal coil, you post a pic to Twitter.[27] Don't make the rookie celebrity mistake of "tastefully" cropping yourself out of the image (or even worse, allowing their death to pass with "respectful silence"). Death is hardest on the living, so assuage your loss with a much-needed PR boost. What the world needs to know is how the passing of this other famous person has affected you. Don't

---

[27] #GoneTooSoon.

feel weird about it. That dead guy from *Star Trek* would've done the exact same thing for you, if you had died.

Casually Adhere Yourself to a High-Profile Thing—If you just come right out and boast on social media, "Oh, I met so-and-so at Something-or-Other magazine's after-party for the Such-and-Such Awards,"[28] it will seem like a blatant grab for attention. Instead, be slightly subtler with that lunge toward relevance—by adopting the classic tack of "How did a goofball/dorkwad/nerdsack like me get invited to this fancy shindig?[29] I sure hope I don't get kicked out! [*False-modesty emoji*]" This serves two purposes: you have successfully reiterated your celebritydom while also over-undermining yourself. Well played.

I Didn't Say It, They Said It (and Then I Shouted It)—The "subtweet" is a great way to spread the self-love while minimizing the shame and greasy after-spread that usually accompanies it. When an admirer, or—better yet—another celebrity, does you a solid by giving you a social media ego stroke, retweet it. But wait—not yet. Let the compliment sit there, seemingly unnoticed, for as long as you can resist (usually three or four hours). Then send the tweet out, but add some qualifying nonsense—"But I thought *you* were the best part of that movie we were both in!"—which, on the surface, seems like a compliment, but is really just you saying,

---

[28] Hosted by Whatshisface, with performances by Blah-blah-blah and Whatever.
[29] Because you yelled at your publicist until you got an invite.

"Yeah, you're right, I'm great, and everyone remember: I appear in movies."

Also, guys? If you'd allow me a rare moment of sincerity: I just want to honestly thank you for reading this silly little book of mine. This is just something I slapped together—more as a goof, really—and the fact that you have dedicated some of your hard-earned free time and money to supporting it is really flattering.[30]

---

[30] Pow! Did you see that? I just nailed that false modesty. I am so fucking good at this.

21

SO MUCH EASIER THAN YOU WOULD ASSUME

HOW TO TURN YOUR ENTIRE LIFE AND CAREER INTO A BOOK THAT PEOPLE CAN BUY AT A GROCERY STORE

O nce you are famous enough, you will have access to many revenue streams. You've got your primary source of income—television acting, movie starring, music making, joke telling, what have you. But there are secondary and tertiary income teats from which to suckle that delicious money-milk. The point is to root around, attempting as many potential cash-in schemes as possible until someone[1] implores you to stop, because you are now embarrassing yourself.

For the modern celebrity, there are a myriad of ways to exploit your fame.[2] You can slap your name on a fragrance, a clothing line, an app, or microwavable breakfast bowls for the professional woman

---

[1] Either a loved one or the buying public.
[2] Which you will refer to as "extending your personal brand," because that sounds less truthful.

on the go.[3] But by far, the easiest way to cash in on your fame is to write a book.[4]

And transforming your personal memories into cash is not as daunting a task as you might assume. Yes, for most famous people, words are scary. And books—which, by definition, can potentially contain dozens of words—are even more frightening.

But they don't have to be. As a celebrity stepping into the world of publishing for the first time, you will be handled very gently. No one is going to expect much from you, which is truly a sweet spot in which to find yourself. The important thing, as a famous person contemplating their first book, is not to try too hard. It's not like you're undertaking some challenging creative endeavor, like starring in a limited-run web series!

Nonfamous aspiring writers might warn you that the book world is just as hard to break into as other parts of the entertainment industry. But they're just jealous and trying to get into your head. For you, securing a book deal will be super easy—because you're a celebrity! People just want to see your face, and potentially your name, in large type—which is why the cover of your eventual book is the most important aspect of the entire writing process.

"But what about the stuff that goes inside the cover—the words and sentences and stuff?" That's a good question—but not an important one. Remember those hangers-on I told you about earlier? Not the sideways-ball-cap guy—he can barely read. No, I mean

---

[3] Joel McHale's She-Meals®!
[4] Clearly.

those two slobs who have written other words for you in the past. *They* can write your book. There—content of book *done*!

So, after the relatively easy step of securing a book deal (and the even easier step of getting someone else to write it for you), you need to figure out what kind of celebrity book you are going to "write." This will inform your eventual book cover.

Luckily, all celebrity memoirs—and their cover designs—fit into one of eight categories:

So THIS Is Thirty?

A FEW MINUTES
OF STAND-UP MATERIAL
**STRETCHED TO
BOOK LENGTH**
THROUGH SHEER
FORCE OF WILL

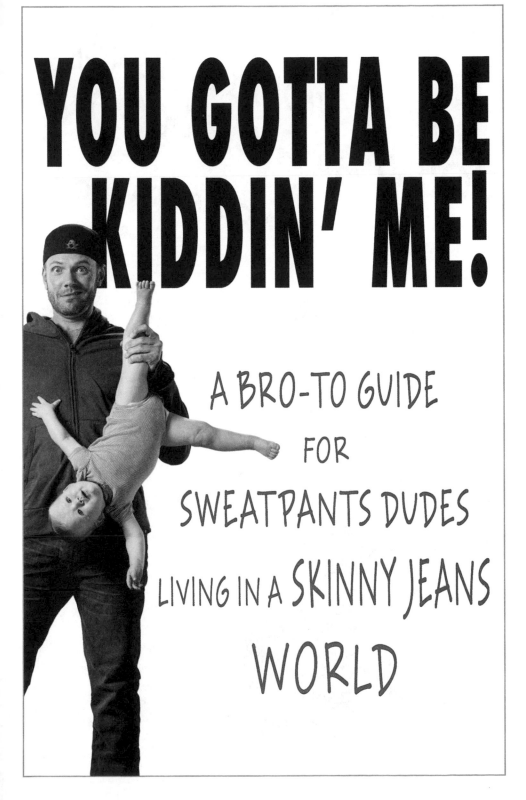

YOU GOTTA BE KIDDIN' ME!

A BRO-TO GUIDE
FOR
SWEATPANTS DUDES
LIVING IN A SKINNY JEANS
WORLD

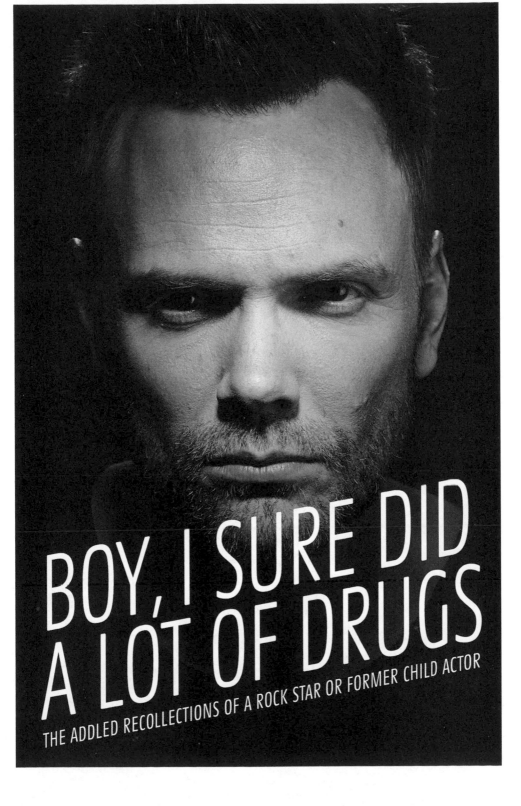

BOY, I SURE DID A LOT OF DRUGS

THE ADDLED RECOLLECTIONS OF A ROCK STAR OR FORMER CHILD ACTOR

MORE BUNS IN THE OVEN

A CELEBRI-MOMMY'S GUIDE TO GLUTEN-FREE BAKING

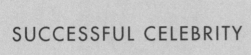

I'M A HUGELY

SUCCESSFUL CELEBRITY

WHO WANTS TO

APPEAR INSECURE

AND RELATABLE

I

——

BROUGHT

——

SNACKS

#MEMOIR

YOU WILL LOL
AT THIS INTERNET
CELEBRITY'S ATTEMPT
TO SPREAD HIS
RELEVANCE BEYOND
A NICHE AUDIENCE

YEP, STILL HERE

AN AGING CELEBRITY
MAKES ONE LAST
CASH GRAB BEFORE
THE GRIM REAPER
SWINGS BY

22

WHY I LEFT SCIENTOLOGY

THE CHAPTER YOU WILL MOST LIKELY JUMP TO WHILE BROWSING IN A STORE

At some point, during the writing process of your tell-all/ self-help/cash-in book, you will arrive at a stunning realization: you are kind of boring. Not as a human being, per se—after all, you are still a celebrity, and attractive, and wealthy, and those elements remain compelling.[1] But your life, arranged as a narrative, now seems slight—and your achievements, viewed in hindsight, appear to be nothing more than the product of hard work, luck, and persistence. This realization will be briefly terrifying—because what I have just described is, in broad terms, the story of *everyone's* life. And I don't know about you, but I don't want to read a book about *you*—I want to read a book about *me*! And you should feel the same way about *you*![2]

So, your life—once compiled and heavily edited by your

---

[1] Enough to "get you in the door," which in the publishing industry equates to the first hundred pages or so of anything you choose to slap your name on.
[2] But mostly *me*!

ghostwriters—needs to be a really good story, so that people will pay money to read it.[3] Think critically. Will your experiences keep an audience flipping those pages? And once you have their cash, does their investment in continuing to flip those pages even matter? This isn't a rhetorical question—I'm actually curious. Like, you don't have to give *refunds* if people hate your book, do you? I keep asking my literary agent about this, and she just acts like she didn't hear me.

Anyway, you really need to think about the entertainment value of your life story, because the inherent juiciness, zesty flavor, and bakery-fresh aroma[4] of your celebrity tale will ensure a healthy advance payment on your book deal. Also, these succulent, tender, irresistible story morsels will drive sales and give you stuff to talk about during the promotional tour.

Think of your favorite movies, or TV shows, or tell-all celebrity biographies—they all share common elements that audiences find compelling.[5] Unfortunately, the average person's life does not contain these things. Your actual experiences probably haven't featured a dastardly villain[6] or crazy action sequences, and—be honest—your sex scenes are most likely boring.[7]

But don't panic. Remember that you are still a famous person, and as such, the bar is already very low for how interesting you must actually be. You're recognizable and marketable—that's how you got

---

[3] Again, thanks for that.
[4] Man, I'm hungry.
[5] With the exception of the feature film adaptation of HBO's *Entourage*.
[6] "Combination skin" doesn't count.
[7] And poorly lit. Get a floor lamp!

a book deal in the first place, silly! Your celebrity memoir will be padded out by the usual lazy celebrity memoir cheats: charts, lists of people you worked with, candid photos from some of your less embarrassing movie and television projects, and maybe even a self-aware chapter or two about the actual writing of the book—you know, *filler*.

You just need a hook—some anecdote or detail that is attention-grabbing or shocking enough to warrant publicity. This will be what puts your book *over the top*.[8] And if you don't have something like this—if your life, when analyzed and forced into a traditional narrative shape, is nothing but some stories about failed auditions, humorous head injuries, and reading disabilities—then you're gonna need to fake some stuff.

Which brings us to a shocking, attention-grabbing, highly promotable event from my life. Feel free to borrow heavily from this when *you* need an exciting anecdote to goose book sales. All I ask is that you change some of the more personal details.[9]

I begin this tale with an exhortation to the more impressionable of you: Please remember, despite the evidence to the contrary glimpsed through my own experiences—and then repackaged in chapters 15 through 21 as "shortcuts to wealth and stardom"—that there are no shortcuts to wealth and stardom. Except for joining a shadowy, pseudo-religious cult.

Let's jump back now, to an earlier time.[10] I was a struggling

---

[8] In terms of book sales, not arm-wrestling tournaments.
[9] And, of course, give me 50 percent of your book's gross receipts.
[10] Like, somewhere between chapters 6 and 7.

actor. Everywhere I looked, I was confronted with billboards touting the high-profile projects of outlandishly successful celebrities: Doug E. Fresh . . . Mimi Rogers . . . Chick Corea.

Certainly *I* could never attain the dizzying heights to which they'd all climbed, in the realms of hip-hop, direct-to-video thrillers, and jazz fusion. But was there *something* that unified them? Something that I, as an impressionable and desperate young artist, could turn to for guidance and a career boost? I wanted to be a real celebrity—I just needed to find some kind of center to help me with this cause. And then I found it: an imposing structure emblazoned with the words "Celebrity Centre."

Inside this building were nice young people wearing impeccable, nautical-inspired clothing. They ushered me into a secret room, where I was administered a "personality test"—and the results were startlingly accurate: I did, indeed, "avoid mean people" and "like things that are nice." It was all so incredibly complex and psychologically incisive. These dead-eyed, inquisitive sailors also seemed very curious about my sexual orientation and surprised me with a pop quiz to see how many films I could name where Kelly Preston appears topless.[11]

Next, they asked what I desired most in life. I said I wanted, in no particular order, fame, wealth, personal fulfillment, free shoes, and the ability to move pens with my thoughts. Incredibly, these Celebrity Centre guides said they could help me achieve every single one of these goals. There was just one catch: we had to begin my

---

[11] They include *Mischief*, *Secret Admirer*, and some brief side-boob in *Jerry Maguire*.

training *immediately*. Oh, and there was one other catch: the dozens of additional, increasingly expensive catches that still lay ahead.

For a simple transaction fee of several thousand dollars, they purified my body with what felt like nothing more than a steam bath and some multivitamins—although I'm certain the regimen was actually more substantial than that. It had to be, for that price!

Then these trustworthy folks explained more about their religious beliefs and how they could help me gain a foothold in Hollywood. The souls clinging to living bodies, the alien jumbo jets, the volcanoes, the galactic overlord who operates in the shadows (all the better to help loyal followers secure roles on *That '70s Show*)—it was everything I knew to be true about the world but was afraid to say out loud, or do any actual research about.

Their leader, like all religious zealots, was a fascinating and charismatic man with horrendous teeth. His solution to achieving wealth, fame, and eternal life seemed so simple that I almost couldn't believe it: surrender tens of thousands of dollars, sign a billion-year contract, and just like that—you're a star![12] I would also be able to talk to animals, rescue people involved in staged public-relations-friendly car accidents, and do tons of other shit.

One afternoon, while gripping two soup cans that these people insisted were some sort of lie detector, I had a vision. I saw my future career stretching out before me—a long and winding path that involved dizzying success, millions of dollars drained from my bank account, and a really awkward sit-down with Matt Lauer. I sud-

---

[12] Of *Swimfan*.

denly snapped back to reality: this wacky "religion" would indeed be my path to fame and notoriety . . . once I escaped from its clutches. This was what my career—and my eventual tell-all book—really needed: a daring escape from an insidious, vindictive cult![13]

So I grabbed the goofy soup can machine and bashed the test administrator across the face. He crumpled to the floor, shouting one of their ancient incantations: "Ow—*my fucking face!*" I darted for the exit. *Ping-ping-ping!* Hundreds of ballpoint pens were being telepathically launched at me. *Thunk-thunk!* The pens narrowly missed me, lodging themselves in the wall. As I rounded a corner, one last pen buried itself in the groin of an L. Ron Hubbard portrait. "Ha ha, right in his dick!" I giggled.

Suddenly, I was tackled from behind by *Walker, Texas Ranger* cocreator Paul Haggis and *King of Queens* wife Leah Remini.

"You could've made some kind of 'pen is mightier' joke," Paul Haggis sneered. "That's what I would've done, and I will someday win an Oscar for writing 2004's *Crash*."

Leah Remini leaned in, her breath hot on my neck. "The soup cans have foretold it," she rasped. "There is no escape for you, Suppressive Person . . ."

They had me pinned against the Celebrity Centre's complimentary breakfast buffet. Leah Remini is freakishly strong, and she pressed my face against a chafing dish of lukewarm sausage links, her claws around my throat. "Surrender, surrender . . ."

I gasped for air, beginning to lose consciousness. I had to escape

---

[13] They are also extremely litigious, so perhaps I should also point out that, maybe, they are a tad misunderstood.

from these liars, these charlatans—before it was too late. So I summoned my courage and used my Scientology powers. Closing my eyes, I reached out—telepathically—to all animals within an eight-block radius. "Hear me, my woodland compatriots . . . hear *meeee* . . ."

"Weak-minded fool!" Paul Haggis bellowed. "Only *we* have the power to . . . what is that noise?" An ominous rumbling arose from outside—the collective footfalls and wing-beats of a veritable army!

The Celebrity Centre's massive, two-story-high stained-glass window—depicting the filming of *Battlefield Earth*'s DVD bonus content—exploded in a hail of glass. Hundreds of animals swarmed inside, summoned by my mind's distress signal.

Chaos descended upon the Scientologists. I glanced around the room, quickly surveying the carnage. I saw Kirstie Alley set upon by a swarm of mandrills, disappearing into a crimson mist . . . Jason Lee remained conscious as several dozen hissing squirrels feasted upon his intestines . . . and Jenna Elfman's impaled form hung limply from the blood-soaked antlers of a Kashmir stag.

I turned to see my attackers—Paul Haggis and Leah Remini—cowering in mortal terror behind a stack of *Dianetics* books as a slavering timber wolf closed in for the kill.

"Stand down, noble friend," I thought toward the wolf, casually waving him aside.

The beast turned his attention to the lady who does the voice of Bart Simpson, biting into her golden throat with a sickening crunch.

"*Ay caramba* indeed," I whispered.

I closed my eyes and—using my most recent Scientology lessons—fired two invisible, psychokinetic mind-bullets at Haggis and Remini. These were *time-release* mind-bullets that would, one day, provide Paul and Leah with the mental fortitude to flee Scientology. I nodded sagely to them both, murmuring, "See you on the best-seller rack."

Then I grabbed as many waffles as I could from the overturned buffet and ran for the exit—leaping over the skeleton of Beck, whose flesh had been stripped clean by a swarm of angrily bubbling jellyfish.

I stumbled into the blinding midday light of a Los Angeles afternoon as fire consumed the Celebrity Centre. I breathed a sigh of relief. I was free.

And I had an amazing story to one day opportunistically recount in my memoir—plus, two mornings' worth of free waffles.

LEAVE 'EM WANTING MORE

HOW TO GET AHEAD OF YOURSELF AND
SET UP YOUR OWN INEVITABLE SEQUEL

As we reach the end of our time together, you may still have one lingering question: how does it all end? In terms of your own experiences, I really don't know.[1] Even my own life as a wealthy, famous person is—as of this edition of the book, anyway—still in progress.

As I have explained, and you will soon learn firsthand, the life of a celebrity is like a roller coaster—plenty of ups and downs, and with a fair share of vomit. And as with any decent roller coaster, people will giddily line up for a second ride. This is a concept you must rely on, and shamelessly capitalize on, as an entertainer: repeat business. Everything you do—your passion projects, your quickie cash-in jobs, your family-dining restaurant-chain investments—should be built for maximal franchisization.

No one thing can be just one thing anymore. As soon as you

---

[1] I don't even know how this *book* is going to end, since, like you, this is the first time I've actually read it.

unveil your latest creative endeavor, you must have—waiting on deck—subsequent, moderately less creative endeavors in the same mold. Sequels, prequels, reboots, deboots—you need to be prepared to reward your audience with ancillary offshoots until they don't even remember what the *original* thing was or why they even liked it in the first place.

"But how am I supposed to sequelize my own life, Joel? Through time travel?" Your question is a tricky one—and not only because a viable means of traversing freely through time has yet to be perfected. Your query is challenging because it requires me to spoil some of the upcoming events in my life and career—and I was expressly saving that material for use in my second book. Plus, your question would lead me into a *bonus* self-help lesson, which I was also tempted to save for the second book.

But you know what? You've been a wonderfully attentive reader, so I will give you one final lesson. What I am about to do is just another form of Hollywood teasing—like the post-credits scene from a superhero movie, where a character shows up whom only your boyfriend, and maybe three other dorks in the theater, actually recognizes from the movie's obscure source material. I am willing to give you an advance peek at what lies ahead for me, Joel McHale, because this may prove useful as you contemplate the next installment of the wildly successful celebrity life you now enjoy.[2]

I expect the next portion of my life, like all sequels, to be bigger, darker, and feature a much larger CGI effects budget. Other than that, it'll be most of the same cast, plus all the jokes and catch-

---

[2] You're welcome, by the way.

phrases that landed the first time.[3] Now, we're in tricky territory here, since this next stuff is all theoretical to me. I am not dead or even retired[4] yet, so even I don't know what wild adventures and fad diets lie ahead. But trust in this: whatever occurs next for me also likely awaits you. And it will all definitely be included in my follow-up book.

Oh, sure. You probably think I've included every juicy celebrity anecdote, every hilarious head injury, every single interesting thing from my life in the pages you now hold—but that's only because that was how this book was marketed to you, silly!

My friends, I have so much more to offer. And it can all be yours, if you buy enough copies of this book to guarantee that a second book will soon be available for you to also purchase.

A Partial List of Really Juicy Personal Stuff That I'm Withholding for My Second Book

- Only the grossest and most detailed of my many troubling sexual predilections
- The nuclear launch codes whispered in my ear by President Obama
- The exact post-tax amount I was paid for each of my acting roles and commercial endorsements[5]
- All the awful things an A-list celebrity told me in confidence, after I was sworn to secrecy[6]

---

[3] "I *still* have diarrhea."
[4] Or shamed into seclusion!
[5] Just kidding, I don't pay taxes. And I'll teach you how to do that, too!
[6] Sorry, Duchovny, I had my fingers crossed that whole time!

- Ryan Seacrest's recipe for a smoothie that grants immortality[7]
- Some other boring shit about my wife and kids, for "lady readers"

Plus! As an added bonus, my next book will provide even more self-help lessons for you to apply to the "back nine" of your own career as a big-time celebrity!

I Never Thought They Would Actually Listen: *How to Win Back the Public After Your First Self-Help Book Resulted in Numerous Deaths*

Come Over Here and Give Grandpappy a Kiss: *How to Assist Hollywood Casting Directors in Selecting Your Increasingly Age-Inappropriate Love Interests*

The Walls Have Ears and the Dog Is Telling Me Secrets: *How to Spin Your Inexhaustible Wealth and Isolation into a Productive Side Career as a Paranoid Weirdo*

Because Nobody Can Tell You No and You're Bored: *How to Select the Heinrich Himmler Biopic That Will End Your Career*

Untouchable and Bulletproof: *How to Enjoy the Wildly Irresponsible Hobbies That Will Lead to Your Embarrassing Death*

- Featuring an in-depth exploration of *knives*—my favorite collectible substitute phalluses!

---

[7] First ingredient: three tablespoons of enchanted sand from the tomb of Imhotep. I've already said too much.

"How did you just do that?" you may be wondering. "How did you sneak what is essentially a commercial for a nonexistent book into an actual book that I paid money for?" Ah-ah-ahh . . . nice try, kiddo. You were just trying to wrest a bonus self-help lesson from me! Your commitment to knowledge and incessant attempts at getting your money's worth from this book are both appreciated and adorable![8]

. . . All right, okay—I will give you one final *final* lesson, and then I will hand you this cup of cocoa and send you off to bed.[9]

At the end of the day, and at the end of this book, the only thing I can really tell you is that, clearly, we are all just making this up as we go. The best advice I can give—no matter your job, your goals, or your true passion in life—is to work hard and try not to take anything too seriously. Do what makes you happy,[10] be a decent human being, and, whenever possible, always ask for the cash equivalent if someone tries to pay you with free luxury items.

And that's about all I got. Thanks for your time and your attention, and as always, thanks for the money.

---

[8] And all for naught, since the book is pretty much over now.

[9] I really should have pointed out this delicious mug of cocoa that I prepared for you right before you started reading. It's gotten pretty cold by now.

[10] Unless it's murder.

EPILOGUE

HERE'S HOW THAT POOL THING SHOOK OUT

The author, seen here with the gradient-depth pool that your
book purchase indirectly helped him renovate.

POST-EPILOGUE
POST-CREDITS SCENE

I toweled off and stepped into my study. The sounds of Boy 1 and Other Boy splashing in the luxuriant multiple depths of our freshly poured pool still echoed in my ears. I had done it—I had gotten two idiots to write a book for me, and that book had helped pay for a slightly deeper pool. I smiled wearily. And there it was, that old feeling again—*satisfaction*—threatening to hold me back from whatever challenge came next.

"Mr. Joel?" It was my manservant, Mateo, standing in the doorway of the study, looking impeccable in his dress whites and matching beret. "You have . . . a visitor?"

I sighed. "Not tonight, Mateo. Just tell them I can't be bothered. Tell them . . . I have diarrhea."

A voice purred, seeming to emanate from within the shelves of my bookcase. "Really? You're gonna bust out that tired old catchphrase of yours . . . on a friend?" The bookcase shifted, before my very eyes, to reveal . . .

"Ryan Seacrest," I scoffed. "When exactly did we become friends?"

"I'd say . . . right around the time you wrote that little book of yours." Seacrest casually removed the dinner jacket onto which he had painted an exact replica of my bookcase shelves—the perfect camouflage. He had been here all along. Always working the angles, blending in . . . this guy was good. "People like us, we need to stick together, Joel . . . for what's coming."

"Oh?" I replied, dismissing Mateo with a quick flick of my middle finger—another one of our classic inside jokes. "And what's coming, Frodo? Another *New Year's Rockin' Eve*?"

Seacrest chuckled as he poured himself a snifter of brandy. "Always with the jokes, right, buddy? Your little . . . memoir–slash–self-help book?" He let the inherent ludicrousness of my book's very concept hang in the air for several seconds. "Did you really think you could just give away all those secrets, without blowback?"

"What are you talking about? My book had charts, and stupid pictures, and a bunch of Chevy Chase anecdotes that I'm pretty sure I just dreamed. Who could possibly—"

"The Whispering Orchid, Joel." Seacrest cocked his head at me, narrowing his eyes. "Oh, what? No jokes?"

And then I heard it—the massive roar of quadruple-turbine engines as the *Revenger*, Ryan Seacrest's personal hover-jet, glided to a soft landing on the grounds of my home, which is a collection of fancy words for "lawn." My hands clenched into fists. "So when do we start?"

"We already have," Seacrest replied, and downed the rest of his brandy.

I took one final look at my sons frolicking in our new pool. I guess *satisfaction* . . . would have to wait.

JOEL McHALE
WILL RETURN

ACKNOWLEDGMENTS

Thank you to Kerri Kolen and everyone at G. P. Putnam's Sons, for seeing the promise of a semicoherent book within the fever dream scrawls of a madman. Thanks also to each of the Putnam's sons, except for Kyle. He knows what he did.

Erin Malone at WME is entitled to 15% of my book-based income, and 100% of my gratitude, for her counsel and guidance.

Additional thanks to my non-literary agents at WME, all of whom nodded dismissively when I mentioned this project, before quickly changing the subject.

Many thanks to the formidable Lewis Kay and Carly Morgan at Kovert Creative, for their vigorous, attentive, and ultimately tender publicizing.

My thanks to Monica Benalcazar at Putnam, and everyone who contributed to the design of the book: Stephen Brayda, Meighan Cavanaugh, Chloe Heyman, and Claire Vaccaro.

Also, much appreciation to F. Scott Schafer, for truly giving an F and shooting beautiful cover images, and interior photos, of a genuinely breath-taking subject.

And thanks to Scott's team: Rick Viars, Kai Lillie, Peter Gargagliano, Scott Stone, and everyone else who assisted with the shoot. I appreciate you not taking too many surreptitious selfies with my bare ass, for that one photo we did not use.

Thank you José Camilo, Pam Lljubo-O'Brien, and Jade Perry for tucking, buffing, shellacking, and making me look great(er) all these years, and also for the year it took to capture the photos for this book.

Jordan Anthony, Sabrina Giglio, and Christina Raquel worked tirelessly to secure media conglomerate-owned photos of my topless body. Matt Carmody put Sean Penn's mustache on a humanoid insect. Ross Beeley provided greatly discounted Seattle photography. Matt Vescovo crafted indelible imagery of me assaulting Chevy Chase. My sincere appreciation to all.

Finally, and most crucially, I must thank the following loved ones—without whom this book (and in some cases, me) would not exist.

To my amazing wife, Sarah—thank you for your love and patience, and for fact-checking my horrible memory. You have given me support, guidance, and two amazing children—so you know what? Go ahead and pick out those fancy outlet covers you had your eye on. You've earned them.

To my sons, Eddie and Isaac—your existence, and the financial pressures contained therein, were a large motivating factor in Daddy "extending his brand" through the written word. Your energy, enthusiasm, and constant, gnawing need for food and shelter have been my guiding light.

To my parents, Laurie and Jack—thank you for your good humor and your rock solid genetic material. You gave me life, you encouraged a thoroughly dumb career choice, and, most importantly, you let me re-imagine your sex lives as comedic book fodder. That was great of you.

To my brothers, Chris and Stephen—thank you for an adolescence filled with danger, an adulthood full of loving extended families, and for allowing me to reduce your personalities to broad caricatures for entertainment purposes.

I sincerely hope I have not forgotten anyone. If I did, it's only because these acknowledgments were actually written by Brad Stevens and Boyd Vico. So blame them. And thanks to them, for writing this entire book or whatever.

PHOTO CREDITS

Original photographs: F. Scott Schafer

Page 17 Personal photos: McHale family

Page 41 Pike Place Market and coffee establishment photos: Ross Beeley

Page 42 CN Tower; tossed salad; scrambled eggs: iStock Photo

Page 48 UW Football photo: University of Washington Photo Vault

Page 50 "Acting Bug" illustration: Matt Carmody

Page 50 Wedding photo: McHale family

Pages 81, 82, 83, 84, 85 Raw meat; actors waiting; ground meat;

cameraman on set; meat blending; executives talking; sausage linking; sausages grilling: iStock Photo

Pages 81, 82, 84, 85   Joel head photos: F. Scott Schafer

Page 84   *The Great Indoors* cast photo: ©2016 CBS Broadcasting Inc. All Rights Reserved.

Pages 91 and 96   *The Soup* and *Community* set photos: Joel McHale

Pages 135, 136, 137, 138, 139   Lips; skull and crossbones: iStock Photo

Pages 157 and 169   Photos from 2014 White House Correspondents' Dinner: J.M. Eddins Jr. Photography

Pages 162, 163, 164, 165   Family photos: McHale family

Page 170   *Sons of Anarchy* © 2012 Twentieth Century Fox Television. All rights Reserved.

Page 170   *Community* courtesy of Sony Pictures Television

Page 170   *Ted:* Photo from the motion picture *Ted* appears courtesy of MRC II Distribution Company L.P.

Page 170   *Adult Beginners*: Brother's Keeper Productions LLC / "Adult Beginners"

PHOTO CREDITS